WHEN MISERY
IS COMPANY

WHEN MISERY IS COMPANY

End Self-Sabotage and Become Content

Anne Katherine

■ HAZELDEN®

Hazelden
Center City, Minnesota 55012-0176

1-800-328-0094
1-651-213-4590 (Fax)
www.hazelden.org

ISBN: 1-59285-084-7

Library of Congress Cataloging-in-Publication Data
Katherine, Anne.
      When misery is company : end self-sabotage and become content /
Anne Katherine.
         p. cm.
      Includes bibliographical references and index.
      ISBN 1-59285-084-7 (softcover)
      1. Self-defeating behavior. 2. Happiness. 3. Self-actualization
(Psychology) 4. Compulsive behavior—Patients—Rehabilitation.
5. Addicts—Rehabilitation. I. Title.
RC455.4.S43K38 2004
158.1—dc22
                                                    2003057130

Author's note
This publication is intended to provide authoritative and accurate information
and is up-to-date and timely as of its date of publication; however, it is not
meant to replace the services of a trained professional, therapy group, or recovery group. This book is sold with the understanding that the publisher and
author are not rendering individual psychological services, or individual services of any kind, to the reader. Should such services be necessary, please consult an appropriate professional.

   The great majority of the examples in this book are true experiences of my
clients, accurately presented (although, to provide anonymity, in all cases I
have changed people's names, and in some cases I have altered potentially
identifying details). In all such cases I have requested and received explicit permission to include people's stories. In a handful of cases, when I did not have a
good real-life example, I have created composite people and situations or (in
very few cases) created fictional people and situations.

   It is important to note that throughout this book, I alternate between using
"she" and "he" to facilitate ease of reading. Nearly every example fits either
gender.

08 07 06 05 04   6 5 4 3 2 1

Cover design by Theresa Gedig
Interior design by Rachel Holscher
Typesetting by Stanton Publication Services, Inc.

TO

Uncle Bud
(Charles Edward Wolflin)
Beloved uncle, a man of true and sterling goodness

Susanne and Tom Stein
Who carry cousinship to a pampered level of generosity and spirit

Jill and Kevin Shea
Thanksgiving for a friendship that deepens every year

And, of course,

Sherry Ascher
For treating my writing as a Real Job

Contents

Part 2: Finding and Living the Solution

Appendixes

ACKNOWLEDGMENTS

My heartfelt thanks to

Christine Lockhart
Who keeps my practice, and my life, intact,
for her dedication to our dreams, her soul, her wisdom,
and her cheesecake

Scott Edelstein
Who always knows how to push open the gates to the muse
and who's the best red-pencil-wielder in the world

Cody Sontag
For letting me adopt her and giving me the experience of being mothered

Pat Matthews and Sherry Buckner
For such big hearts and openhanded giving,
both as playmates and in embracing the vision of Avonlea

Rabbitt Boyer
For friendship, generosity, and honor

Ann Weston, Karen Selby, Judy Burns, and Cassie Major
Because I wouldn't be here now if you hadn't been there way back when

To the Cove OH and Poker Society
Harry Lynam and Barbara Self
For endless games of Oh Hell, poker, and euchre,
and for showing up when something is tough

Blaine Haigh, Bridgemobile Captain
For rescuing me on a routine basis and
Joan Haigh
An endless source of good reading, manna for an author

Wauneta Fortson (Ace)
For many fun, good evenings at my wonderful table,
but please, quit leading trump, and
Gloria Tarver
Eternal mother, wise, warm, and generous

Avonlea Advisors and Board Members
For creating a haven community for women
who have carried too many tears, and
Avonlea Community Members
For having the courage to try one more thing

PART ONE

Understanding the Problem

CHAPTER ONE

Can This Book Really Help?

Carrie left me a message. "I'm scared. My new office was finished yesterday, so I moved into it today. It's really beautiful, with a view of the ships' canal. My new boss likes me a lot. This morning she asked me to join some of the managers at an informal dinner at her home tonight. I accepted and got directions.

"I hadn't eaten breakfast and then I worked through lunch. After work, I went into the ladies' room and looked at myself and I thought, *How could anyone believe in me? I'm gross looking. My clothes are all wrong.*

"So I putzed around, arranging my office, and lost track of the time and left fifteen minutes late. And then I got stuck behind a school bus. So I got to her place thirty minutes late. And then I saw the house she lives in. It's huge. It's elegant. What was I doing there?

"And all the cars were there already. Nobody was still arriving. I sat outside for an hour and I couldn't make myself go in. So I finally just left. I went to a restaurant and ate about three meals. Then I came home.

"I'm not good enough for this kind of job. I was afraid I would do some stupid thing if I went inside and that everyone would hate me. And that she'd think she made a big mistake hiring me."

I closed my eyes as I heard this because I could see the series of actions and nonactions that became a cascade of self-sabotage for Carrie. I could tell she wasn't seeing how her failure to show up would come across to her boss. In the state she was in, she couldn't imagine what would be happening inside the house—her boss and the managers waiting for her, delaying dinner, wondering and worrying, then waiting for an explanatory phone call. She'd gotten lost in a tunnel in her head and saw everything from inside out.

At first it seemed to me that the trigger—the first event that started her slide—was seeing herself in the ladies' room mirror. But her anxiety had been brewing before that. Her fancy new office scared her. Her boss's appreciation scared her. Even her own thoughts scared her—what if she couldn't measure up? The invitation to be a member of the inner circle may have been the final straw.

So much bounty so soon in her new job led her to fear that she might not rise to others' expectations. This fear caused her to see herself as unattractive when she looked in the mirror.

Carrie had already put herself in danger of not thinking clearly by skipping breakfast and lunch. Then she made a series of decisions—or, rather, failed to make decisions—that could have led to a better outcome. She putzed instead of thinking about how to get ready, didn't set an alarm in order to get out of the office on time, and didn't call a therapy group member to get help with her anxiety and decisions. By not acting in an effective way, she allowed the internal avalanche to build.

By the time she was sitting outside her boss's elegant home, she was in too deep. She had been swallowed by her anxiety and couldn't think clearly enough to figure out how to ring the doorbell and go inside. Her world had gotten very small; at that moment it consisted entirely of her fears and that big, imposing house. Eventually I realized that I had my eye on the wrong thing too. I wanted Carrie to keep that job and the support of her boss. I wanted her to succeed in her profession and have enough money to allay her financial worries. I wanted very much for her to not rack up another failure. I wanted her to be happy.

Many years of being a therapist had honed my ability to work effectively with people. But in Carrie's case I was operating under a wrong assumption. I believed she wanted to be happy.

I was missing the paradox. For some people, happiness is upsetting. For them, every joy must be equalized by a setback. Too much success must be balanced by failure.

COMFORT IN MISERY

We are creatures of survival. We were biologically designed, engineered, and programmed to survive, more or less, at all costs. Yet survival can carry many faces. If, for whatever reason, misery seems necessary for our survival, we'll choose misery.

Simplified, the logic goes like this:

Something good happened to me→I was happy→Then this horrible thing followed or came from the same place or person that made me happy→I was nearly crushed by my grief. This means that happiness leads to crushing grief→Therefore, if I avoid happiness, I'll protect myself from grief.

Different people might substitute other words for *happy,* such as *safe, joyful, free,* or *honored.* Or they might use other words for *grief,* such as *fear, disappointment, shame,* or *disaster.* For example, *I felt so special as they sang "Happy Birthday" to me. Then my father slapped me out of the chair, and I nearly died from shame. So if I can avoid being honored, I'll protect myself from shame.*

In all of these cases, the internal logic is the same: people try to protect themselves against feeling bad by not feeling too good.

TRIGGERED BY JOY

A triggering event is one that sets off an inevitable chain reaction. To trigger all the dominoes to fall, tip the first domino. To trigger yeast to grow, add water and sugar.

Abstinent, recovering food addicts can get triggered by one cookie. It may take an hour or a week for the relapse to take hold, but the trigger is the first bite. From then on, for most sugar addicts, the slide into relapse is inevitable.

For some of us, happiness itself can be a trigger, a trigger that makes a slide into misery equally inevitable. In Carrie's case, she was triggered by a symbol of success, her boss's appreciation and an invitation into the inner circle. These were positive, exciting possibilities, and Carrie recognized them as such. But that recognition caused a surge of anxiety for Carrie, and she ended up handling that anxiety by behaving in a way that made her unhappy—and made others unhappy with her.

ENSURING MISERY

On the surface, Brian's pattern seemed quite different. Though he hated hospitals, he worked as an orderly. He had a quick wit and an intelligent mind but stopped attending his advanced training program at the community college even though the course was interesting, his instructor was good, and the program could have led to a better job with more money.

He lived in a dank, bare studio apartment that he hadn't made comfortable. He dated women he did not love or even like. Nothing in life entranced him. He plodded from requirement to requirement without being engaged.

He seemed to have an instinct for making choices that would keep him at that same dutiful, empty level of existence. If he needed to turn left to take the only available parking space, he'd turn right.

When a coworker lovingly teased him, Brian took offense and chewed her out so harshly that the coworker, who had been taking some first steps toward an offer of friendship, decided not to pursue it.

Brian was so afraid of happiness that he made sure he was always miserable.

Brian and Carrie lead very different lives. Brian's life is colorless and dark. Carrie is successful, and she has reason to be happy. But both keep making choices that maintain them at a carefully calibrated level of existence—beneath bliss and above despair.

A LARGER ADDICTION

Sugar made Stephanie fearful and listless. If she took a bite of a doughnut or two swigs of cola, within forty-eight hours she would be eating sugary foods addictively. Her whole focus would switch to her next bite—where, when, and how she'd get a new stash of sugar and eat it. She would be distracted from work and her relationships.

When she abstained from sugar, Stephanie was clearheaded, made positive choices, and felt good. All aspects of her life improved.

Through concentrated attention and effort, she stayed abstinent from sugar for seven months. Then she sent me an e-mail: "I lost my abstinence."

My heart groaned. I knew what would happen next. She was headed for a downhill slide in which she would binge on sugar more and more and feel ever worse about herself. Her abstinence had been hard-won. It would not be easily regained.

Was she just a typical addict, I wondered, with the typical propensity for relapse? Or was something larger going on?

Among addicts of any stripe—alcoholics, drug addicts, food addicts, compulsive workers—some achieve a level of recovery in which their lives gradually improve and become more fulfilling. And there are others who relapse again and again.

In some cases, the addiction has too firm a hold. The addict seemingly cannot become reconciled to a life without his addiction.

But there's another category of people who relapse. These are the people *who are triggered by recovery itself*. They are also the people who we helping professionals have failed to help.

Recovery brings clarity, friendships, and joy. It draws people into union with life. Serendipity shows up, again and again.

For some addicts, this is too much of a good thing.

Why? Because a bigger addiction, a more powerful and more subtle addiction, is pulling the strings—an addiction to misery.

It's a subtle addiction that has many faces, but the common thread is this: when things go too well or the person feels too good, she sabotages herself in order to return to the more comfortable or familiar state of misery, unhappiness, or grayness. In some cases, the mere *possibility* that things might go well or that good feelings might arise is enough to trigger behavior that brings back the misery.

Brian nips joy in the bud. Carrie hacks at it after it's been growing a while. Stephanie lets her food addiction pull her back under.

The experiences of these three people look different, but the bottom line is the same. Not one of them realizes that they are sabotaging themselves. They don't wake up in the morning, stretch, and say, "Life is getting too wonderful. I think I'll spoil it today."

Instead, at some point they cross a critical line that causes anxiety or fear or unease to build. This transition is difficult for them (and, usually, anyone else) to notice. But once that line is crossed, they move into behavior that attempts to discharge the anxiety.

Yet, because they are focused on getting rid of their painful feelings, they don't perceive the other consequences of their behavior. The good things or feelings that were present become altered as a result. And with the removal of those good things, their anxiety diminishes. Even if the loss of what was good is upsetting, that condition is more bearable than their former anxiety.

For some of us, feeling too good for too long (or even feeling good at all) is scary. Achievement creates anxiety. Intimacy leads to fear. Happiness produces discomfort. Pleasure causes pain. The solution to this dilemma: what feels good has to be stopped.

I call this an addiction to misery. For some people, it might be more appropriate to talk about an addiction to victimization, or unhappiness, or failure, or being failed by others.

This book provides an introduction to this problem and a practical program for climbing out of it.

HOW THIS BOOK CAN HELP

This book is for people who suspect they suffer from an addiction to misery but don't know how they got there or what to do about it.

It's also for the families and loved ones of these people, who have been puzzled by the destructive choices they've watched their friends, partners, or family members make.

An addiction to misery is a particularly pernicious and difficult problem because it operates behind the scenes like a puppeteer behind a curtain. It can manifest in so many guises that the larger pattern can be easy to miss. Maybe you have read books on codependency or related recovery issues, yet you didn't find solutions for yourself. This could be the reason: a larger, hidden issue was actually going on that was influencing you.

It is not unsolvable. The program in this book offers a path to emancipation and a way to expose and neutralize the configuration of events that imprinted the problem in the first place.

I've watched and exulted as my own clients have used this program to protect or improve their jobs, restore their health, find intimacy, and collapse in unfettered, uproarious laughter and delight.

This is a book of solutions and of hope. It's a way to empower yourself to step beyond the invisible web that has held you captive. It's a doorway into a fuller existence.

Welcome.

CHAPTER TWO

The Paradox

Do you want to be happy? Are you longing for powerful intimacy, joyous success, greater fulfillment? Me too.

But do you also fear all of these things a tad? After all, they might not last, and the loss could be more devastating than ever having them.

Actually, most of us fear these things, at least a little bit, out of an instinctive dread of pain. The problem arises when our fear is so strong that it prevents us from going after those things which, deep down, we really want out of life.

This book looks at and resolves a paradox. It presents a program to help people who have a fear of feeling better so that they can begin to feel better.

If, in your heart, you sense that this book is talking about you, then the book places you in a dilemma. As a result, you might want to discredit it. You might get really angry at some things I say. You may want to split hairs to prove that this book isn't talking about you.

I'm proposing a new possibility for you—a way to feel better without feeling so scared. Something happened in your life, probably early on, that crossed some of your wires. As a result, happiness is worrisome for you. Intimacy feels scary. Success is upsetting. Feeling better feels worse. Loneliness feels empty but safe. Mistakes are upsetting but familiar. You are stuck in a twilight zone of unfulfillment—dissatisfied but protected.

I understand this is a terribly complex, difficult issue. You yourself may have been puzzled by the things you do but feel trapped by circumstances and can't see a way out. At times this system you are in may operate like a reflex. Maybe you've surprised yourself by what you've done. You've been shocked when a turn of events comes crashing down. Whatever is at work in you seems to have its own set of batteries, its own control panel. Something deep inside of you that you don't understand is calling the shots.

This book proposes a way out.

It's not a quick fix. It will take ongoing attention. The steps have to be small ones, because if things get too much better too fast, you are likely to be triggered into repeating old, familiar patterns.

As you use this book to change your life, that internal, fearful self may emerge and yell at you to throw this book out the window, or wonder what's the use, or search for the one chapter or paragraph or sentence that doesn't precisely fit so you can discredit the whole book.

A big part of—and a big challenge in—dealing with this problem is maintaining your own awareness of the big picture. It's important to keep your perspective when this fearful inner self says, "See. This author is all wet. She said you would prefer striped wallpaper, and you don't even like wallpaper."

At these points, you can answer, "Okay, I know you. You're the part of me that's scared to have hope. I remember the big picture. I'm more comfortable when things go wrong, and that's why I have these thoughts. I know you're only trying to make my life feel safer, and I appreciate that. But, you know what? It's hurting a lot more than it's helping. I'd like to start acting differently so that I can enjoy feeling good more often."

I'll be talking more about this in a later chapter, but for now you'll need a way to hang on long enough to get that far. So, *right now,* before you do anything else, grab a pen or pencil, and please fill in the following blanks to create a sentence:

I may be _____   _____.

Blank one: (pick one)   Blank two: (pick one)
   addicted to   misery
   more comfortable with   things going wrong
   relieved by   being unhappy
   your words   suffering
                    your words

Jot down this sentence on a scrap of paper, and use it for a bookmark so that you can recall the big picture if you get angry or frightened as you read this book.

MAKING HELP HELPLESS

There is another facet of this problem. When other people try to help you, *you may need for that help to fail.*

It may not feel like this to you from the inside. You may experience it like this:

No one understands.

No one really gets how it feels.

Friends and therapists are missing the boat. They suggest things I can't do. They don't come close to understanding how I see things.

When someone reaches out to you, you may find yourself feeling critical of him. You may start talking to yourself about how his life isn't so perfect. You may see him as arrogant. You may feel trapped, all alone, separated from what you see others enjoying.

Here's the deal. When things start going well, you get afraid. Then, when people try to help you, they almost always suggest things that make you feel more afraid. Then you have to ignore them or push them away to get relief from the pressure they put on you.

If this sounds familiar, I'd like you to stay with this book. I understand that I'll be suggesting things that will scare you. But, deep down, isn't there a part of you that wants deliverance from this problem? Wouldn't it be great to be happy without being afraid? Would it mean something to you to be successful or to be intimate with someone without having to feel anxious or scared?

I congratulate you for reading even this far. As powerful as the inner workings of this self-protection system may be, you must also have some part of you that's longing to heal.

A VICTORY AND A FAILURE

Brittany's mother screwed up big time when Brittany was a kid. She married a drunk who treated Brittany cruelly, but she was too fixated on her own needs to protect or rescue her daughter.

Once Brittany had become a young woman, her mom began to make herself into a different person. She got into recovery and therapy. She freed herself from drunken men. She put herself through school. As she got wiser, she had more to give Brittany, and she started trying to help her.

But Brittany was angry. She had lost two decades of her own life to dead ends and hurtful relationships. She had lived in a deep pattern of disappointed hopes. She could see that her mother now cared for her and was offering amends, but Brittany was so angry that it fulfilled something in her to keep her mom's offers from working.

Her childhood had been horribly thwarted. Now, as an adult, she got a kind of pleasure from thwarting her mother, even at her own expense.

Brittany did try therapy now and then, and she could see that these kind people cared about her. She'd start to receive their help, but then something inside her would rear up, and she'd feel like she had to defeat the therapist.

Of course, it defeated her too. It mangled her therapy. Even therapists, those most patient of souls, lose their steam eventually when they aren't helping. Brittany took a certain satisfaction in wearing a therapist out. It made her feel powerful.

Being powerful enough to keep her mom, and a string of skilled therapists, from helping soothed the powerlessness she felt as a child. Their defeat pleased her anger. It was a way to punish her mother for her severe mistakes.

The therapists were Mother stand-ins. They got punished too, both for caring and for presuming that they could offer anything that could match the suffering Brittany had endured. Their power-lessness only proved how much Brittany's mom had hurt her.

So Brittany was feeding these hidden mouths inside her, but her life was a shambles. Inside, she was suffering much more than the people she was trying to punish. Her vindication at their failures didn't truly make her happy. The scales of justice never truly balanced. The little bit of gratification she got when another friend or therapist went down in defeat was a Pyrrhic victory. No matter how much it cost the other person, her own losses were bigger. It wasn't really what she wanted out of life. The bottom line is this: no one really suffers as much as you do when you need others to fail.

But what can you do if this system seems to act like a reflex, operating on its own, triggered by subtleties you may not even see?

Plenty.

You see, these internal forces can be tended to, expressed, and channeled. *But they do not need to be defeated.*

This is not a book about how to control uncontrollable forces. It's not about ripping out a part of yourself that has for years engineered your survival.

Instead, it's about gathering the tools you will use to save yourself, honoring the behaviors and systems that have helped you to survive so far, then going deeper to meet your truest needs.

PRACTICING THE ART OF WATCHING

If you have an internal reflex that doesn't want this book to work, what can you do to keep going? This: instead of fighting the part of you that resists these ideas, just watch it.

Part 1. Watching Yourself Think

What are you thinking right now? Watch your thoughts. Don't stop them. Don't edit them. Don't argue with them. Just watch them.

For example, I'm thinking about taking a walk. So I notice that I'm thinking about taking a walk. Then I notice that I'm thinking I'm too busy to take a walk. Then I notice that I'm thinking the dog would enjoy taking a walk. Then I remember that I'm waiting for a phone call and I notice remembering that.

Part 2. Watching Yourself Meet a Need

What is a need you have right now? Are you thirsty? Do you need to use the bathroom? Do you need to put on something warmer or cooler?

Get up and notice how you feel as you stand. Begin walking toward the solution to your need. Hear the thoughts in your head as you are moving. Notice how your muscles feel as you walk. Notice how you balance yourself.

As you turn toward the answer to your need, notice what you are looking at. What goes through your mind as you reach for the thing you need? Don't argue with whatever is going on in your mind; just pay attention to your thoughts. Notice how you feel right before you begin doing the thing that will meet your need.

Now, fulfill that need. Drink the water, use the bathroom, or take off the sweater.

Notice what you are thinking, what emotions you are feeling, how your body feels.

When you are done, pay attention to yourself as you go back to what you were doing. Notice how your body feels. Notice your muscles as you move. Notice how you feel about taking care of your need. Notice what you are thinking.

This can become a powerful tool for self-awareness—watching yourself, observing your thoughts.

WATCHING YOURSELF AS YOU READ

When your thoughts start to tell you to get rid of this book, watch them. Notice the fear or anxiety that has been triggered. Go back to what you just read and find the words that started the reflex. Notice what those words mean to you.

Continue watching your thoughts unfold. Don't argue with them; don't negotiate with them. Treat them like elevator music.

Remember the big picture. One way to do this is to photocopy the box on the next page and stick the page into this book. Reread it when your thoughts tell you to put this book aside.

Big Picture

In the past, I tended to reject help.
I'm changing my pattern of resisting help.
I will let myself have the help of this book
so that I can stop sabotaging myself.
When I resist the ideas in this book,
that's the old pattern kicking in.
I notice this and continue.
I will feel better.

Remember: *you* are the one reading this book; *you* are the one making it happen.

You are in control of the process. You can speed it up or slow it down. You can take breaks. You can think. You can make choices. You can remember the big picture.

Your life can be full and happy. You can liberate yourself from the invisible chains that have kept you from moving toward your deepest desires. You can find fulfillment.

You can have happiness without fear.

CHAPTER THREE

What's the Use?

Carrie and Stephanie are addicted to misery. Do they *enjoy* being miserable? No.

Although some people do get an odd kind of happiness or satisfaction out of being unhappy, misery addicts are not usually seeking a state of misery. More likely, they fall into misery by default, as a result of a deeply engrained pattern of choices or behaviors, or blindness to choices.

They are defeated over and over by a fear of risking (translated as losing what little they have) based on an overwhelming feeling that nothing for them can improve or change. Regardless of how they might appear to others, on the inside what they are feeling is, *What's the use? Things can't be different for me. This is all I get to have out of life. I'd better hold on to this because if I let go, I might have nothing at all.*

Drenched in hopelessness, they see no point in using help offered to them. Frozen in fear, they miss deadlines and waste opportunities. On a very basic level, they have given up.

What are they addicted to? The simplest way to put it is this: *misery addicts are addicted to the system they have devised to protect themselves from unbearable disappointment.* To this end, they may have enlisted other addictions or compulsions. These other addictions serve the dual purpose of giving them a sort of comfort and helping them avoid their misery, fear, or hopelessness.

A typical misery addict is surrounded by a constellation of addictions she actively practices. Some of these parallel addictions include food addiction, compulsive shopping, frequent sickness, compulsive working, compulsive gambling, compulsive game playing, computer fantasy games, compulsive exercise, compulsive spending, codependence, excessive caretaking, self-abuse, compulsively depriving oneself of human needs, sleeping too much, sleeping too little, and, of course, the old standbys—addiction to alcohol and other drugs, including nicotine and caffeine.

I call these *tool addictions*. These are addictions used collectively as tools to sustain misery. They are used as levers to escape and soothe—and to cause more misery.

The misery addict may not feel addicted to any of these and may not look addicted to other people because he rotates among them. However, each serves the dual purpose of helping him check out and giving his life a focus.

Even if he is able to admit to an addiction, he typically has terrible trouble sustaining recovery from that addiction. One signal that misery is the true addiction is when someone's efforts to recover from what he sees as his main addiction keep failing.

An example of this can be found in Walt's story. While in recovery from alcoholism, Walt was clear that he was also a workaholic and a food addict. He tried setting schedules, making promises, joining a men's group, and attending Overeaters Anonymous. He'd get some control over his work and his food, and then he'd forget his plan. This happened many times, with a corresponding loss of self-trust and increasing problems with his family.

Recovery from a tool addiction can't work unless the larger, encompassing addiction to misery is also being treated. The tug to sabotage successful recovery and the joy that recovery brings will ultimately intervene.

As Walt's past becomes littered with more and more failures at recovery from these linked addictions, he becomes ever more convinced that he is a failure, doomed to exist outside the stream of living, different and less worthy than others.

Any addiction creates a set of problems common to the other addictions—a tendency to isolate, a life reeling with difficulty (no

Recovery

Recovery means the return to a normal or improved state after an injury or loss. When addiction is the context, the word *recovery* is also used to refer to the process by which this happens.

The largest, most successful recovery program in the world, Alcoholics Anonymous (AA), has brought millions of people out of the despair of alcoholism and into sobriety and joyful living. Many other kinds of addiction have proven to be responsive to the AA program so that numerous spin-offs now exist with the same basic principles. These principles include abstinence (from the addictive substance or behavior), anonymity, a Twelve Step healing process, and a nonjudgmental fellowship in which leadership is passed from member to member. There are no dues or fees, no initiations, and no forms to fill out. There are no supervisors, but volunteer sponsors will give guidance, if asked.

Programs that follow the AA model end in the word *anonymous*, such as Gamblers Anonymous, Narcotics Anonymous, Overeaters Anonymous, and Food Addicts Anonymous. An exception is Al-Anon, which is for people who are close to someone with an addiction.

matter how orderly it looks), secrecy around involvement with the addiction, protecting the addiction, and a mind that thinks it isn't addicted.

With traditional addictions, the source is obvious and the centerpiece of attention—alcohol, pills, slot machines, sugar—stands as the icon for the problem. With an addiction to misery, the nucleus is more subtle. No icon covers it.

The centerpiece for misery addiction is a *system*.

Misery addicts have devised a system by which they've survived crushing disappointment, devastating abandonment, occasions of despair, ongoing separateness from others, overwhelming fear, and ordeals of being misunderstood and misread. Their system has even been powerful enough to withstand the seductive whisperings from their own minds, which tell them that they might as well give up entirely. Misery addicts are addicted to this system because it has saved them from annihilation.

They are also addicted to avoidance. To a certain degree, of course, every addiction promises to take its person away from full consciousness. But a misery addict *needs* avoidance. She craves avoidance the way an alcoholic craves alcohol. This is the service that the shifting addictions provide for a misery addict—a road out of too much consciousness.

This is the reason misery addicts are susceptible to multiple addictions and why they can pick up a new addiction in the blink of an eye. Anything that serves up avoidance may be added to their repertoire. They can go from ignorance of an activity to addictive use of it overnight.

Living in avoidance is one reason that misery addicts sabotage themselves. They take in the world only partially. While they are busily avoiding things, they miss the important announcement; they don't act in time; they aren't seeing the subtle signs that someone could be a friend; they wait too long to make the reservation.

In the absence of complete information, they are vulnerable to their own projections and anxieties and fears. Then they may act on their own thoughts as if those thoughts were reality.

They may not realize the part they've played in bringing about a negative outcome. They may not know they've sabotaged themselves. But the new disappointment gets added to the list. Now they have even more proof that they don't get to be happy.

And this unhappiness must be avoided.

Thus, the cycle continues.

SO WHAT *IS* THE USE?

Your life has value, even if you can't recognize it today. You were born for a reason.

A series of catastrophic events separated you from knowing your true self, and you are now walking around in a suit of armor that you are deeply accustomed to. You don't even realize how heavy it is.

Here are some good reasons for facing and handling this addiction:

1. You owe it to yourself. You deserve to give yourself a chance at recovering your true life.
2. Your true self is missing you. She's lonely. He's lonely.
3. Every year that you put off facing your addiction is another year of your life gone. The sooner you pay attention to these issues, the more you'll be able to really live and experience genuine joy.
4. You'll be healthier. All addictions harm the body in one way or another. The immune system gets all tied up when we operate primarily by defending ourselves. As you heal emotionally, your very cells will breathe easier.
5. An important life lesson (perhaps several) will be revealed and learned as you work in the process of recovery.
6. By learning to access and tolerate feelings of joy and happiness, you'll make more money. As Martin Seligman writes in *Authentic Happiness,* "Research suggests . . . that more happiness actually causes more productivity and higher income."[1]
7. Your goodies are waiting for you. An abundance of joy, intimacy, and fulfillment are sitting on your life's road waiting for you to walk along and pick them up.

CHAPTER FOUR

Tilt

"Fix it, Baby, fix it."

Sammie stopped hitting her tennis ball against the garage and surveyed the scene with her ten-year-old eyes. She gave a very quiet too-adult sigh.

Her mother sat limply on the back stoop, her hand dangling, the jelly glass smashed inches below her hand. The smell of rum slightly overpowered the smell of cola.

Sammie pushed through the screen door and returned with the broom and dustpan. As she swept sparkling glass bits out of the shaggy grass, her mother said, "No, Baby, not yet. Get me another drink first."

When her mother had a fresh glass in hand and Sammie had rinsed off the stoop, her mother put her arm out to the side and said, "Come here, Baby."

Sammie hated to be close to her mother when she reeked of rum and her body went floppy. But Sammie knew from long experience that if she resisted, her mother would swap her teariness for fury and hound her until she complied anyway.

She edged into her mother's side, which was damp from humidity and sweat, trying to keep a bit of air between them, but her mother clamped her like a vise. "I love you, Baby. You are my precious girl. Precious, precious."

Now fast-forward twenty-five years to observe the childhood dilemma imposed on an adult situation (and its effect on a friendship). As Voula and thirty-five-year-old Sammie were taking a walk, Voula said, "It's hard for me to say this, Sammie, but I'm getting tired of waiting for you. You were twenty minutes late today. Last week you were fifteen, and the week before you cancelled just as I was walking out the door. It makes me feel as if our get-togethers aren't that important to you, and I'm getting angry that my time isn't respected."

"I am such a screwup," Sammie replied in a contrite voice. "I know your time is valuable, and our friendship matters a lot to me. I just can't get myself to keep from doing that one extra thing on the way out the door, and then it leads to another, and I suddenly realize I'm late."

"We've talked about this before," Voula said, "but you aren't doing anything different. You say one thing and do another, and not just in this situation. There are things you could do. You could set an alarm to alert yourself. You could program your computer to flash a message."

Voula continued, "I want you to hear that this matters to me. Partly I don't have time to throw away. But even more, I feel blown off when I don't see you taking any measures to make it work out. Next week, I'm waiting five minutes, and then I'm walking whether you are here are not."

"Okay, fair enough. It's a good idea to set an alarm."

Voula gave an explosive sigh. "I feel like a harpy and I don't want to feel like this, but I'm angry. It seems to me that if you valued how upset I was the last couple of times we talked about this, you could have been setting an alarm already."

"You're right. I could have thought of it. I got overwhelmed, feeling like such a loser, and then just checked out on the whole incident."

Voula chose not to say more because it would have seemed like a threat if she'd put her feelings into words, but she knew that if Sammie didn't follow through, it was going to cause her to back off from their relationship.

Sammie had forgotten the previous incidents and hadn't acted on them because each time she had fallen so deeply into shame that she'd drowned her memories in a sugar binge.

Sammie had said many times, and deeply believed, that friendship was exceedingly important to her. This was true. When Sammie was fully present, no one doubted her love or her sincerity when she offered her friendship. But over and over, her behavior did not match either her words or her passionate promises.

Sammie was devastated when she lost a friend and couldn't understand it. She was committed to her friends and fervent in her regard for them. From her point of view, their periodic exodus made no sense. She couldn't fathom why a friend would throw away something as dear as friendship for something so trivial as lateness.

Friends gave up on Sammie, but not just because of lateness or broken commitments. They also quit because they got tired of trying to handle confusion they didn't understand.

When a friend's behavior doesn't match her words, it is confusing and even hurtful.

Sammie created a dilemma for her friends because when she said she would not be late again, her energy was completely in alignment with her words. She was entirely believable because she herself believed and meant what she said.

But after such a convincing promise, when Sammie showed up quite late again, that combination created dissonance for her friends. Did Sammie know she created dissonance in her friends? No. Did she know she had an internal conflict? No. Was there a consequence for someone? Yes, for her friends, until they protected themselves by leaving—and for Sammie after they left. Eventually, even her fervent promises and plausible excuses wouldn't cut it anymore.

Sammie exhibited a common theme among misery addicts: a longing for intimacy matched by a fear of intimacy.

If we draw a line with longing for intimacy at one end and fear of it at the other, there's some point at which we come to a balance for ourselves, where our longing is tempered by our fear.

FEAR		LONGING
LOW	DEGREE OF INTIMACY	HIGH

This point comes close to the amount of intimacy we can tolerate without getting so afraid that we must do something to distance ourselves from the other person.

When Sammie was with a friend, the reality of the person in front of her dissipated her fear, and she could fully participate. But before meeting with a friend, a nameless, unfelt fear of getting hurt by intimacy led her to get distracted by various tasks. When she was at home or work, the reality of that friend receded, to be replaced with a vague image of a loved one who took instead of gave and who forced her into unpleasant contact. This image was not conscious but stirred deep inside of her.

Sammie felt this dissonance and did not know it, and she passed on this dissonance to her friends. They did not comprehend or name it, but they experienced it, and eventually it eroded their relationships with Sammie.

If we go back in time, we can see that Sammie's mother created dissonance for Sammie. She made her daughter fix problems she herself created; she pretended to give while taking; and she forced unpleasant physical contact in the name of love. Sammie grew up with an emptiness, with a yearning for profound connection with others. She also had embedded in her, like a time bomb, a profound fear of being engulfed and used in the name of love. This conflict flowered in her behavior and set the course of her relationships.

The following theme, and its many variations, can be found throughout the lives of misery addicts: *a longing for success and unconscious acts that keep it at bay.* The misery addict yearns for happiness and sets up sadness, wants financial security and repeatedly sabotages financial plans, desires family but keeps potential family at a distance, wants meaningful work but keeps busy with work that won't ever go in the desired direction. Thus the longing for happiness never shrinks, and the efforts to attain it rarely succeed.

CHAPTER FIVE

The Horns of the Dilemma

Recovering from an addiction to misery demands a type of care and precision not always required in other addiction recovery programs.

All recovery programs are about getting into right relationship with yourself and others. Yet, with every addiction, at least one thing about recovery is difficult and one thing is easy. For example, recovery from alcohol addiction is difficult because if you slip once, you might never crawl out of the bottle again. One drink can kill you. Food addiction is easier in that respect because one wrong bite is not likely to kill you.

On the other hand, an alcoholic can stay away from alcohol in a way that a food addict can never hope for. An alcoholic doesn't have to sit down with his demon three times a day.

In most of the common addictions, our first task is to separate ourselves from the addictive behavior by becoming abstinent. The first days and weeks of abstinence are a serious challenge because we experience the discomfort of withdrawal. Thus simply achieving abstinence is a job in itself.

Once we're past withdrawal, our next challenge is to learn to live differently. By getting others' support, going to meetings, and keeping ourselves in contact with recovering people, we can take whatever time we need to refine our manner of living. Both tasks—getting abstinent and altering one's manner of living—are challenging, but we don't have to do both tasks all at once.

With an addiction to misery, however, it's the manner of living itself that is the problem.

Abstinence is clear-cut with alcohol, drug, and food addiction. You don't drink, use drugs, or eat addictive foods.

But what is abstinence with misery addiction? After all, misery addicts are addicted to a system—the system they've used to survive.

It's standard for us recovery professionals to say that we can't work with someone's personal history until he is in recovery. As long as a person is drinking or using other drugs, he isn't clear enough to do therapy. Even a compulsive gambler, food addict, or codependent will have limited success with therapy as long as he is practicing his addictions.

For a misery addict, though, the injuries of childhood are part and parcel of the entire addiction. The addiction typically begins with early trauma, which results in incomplete life and relationship skills, which in turn create more trauma as a result of the person being unskilled and unconscious of the addiction. Add to this the problems created by the tool addictions, and the misery addict has a big task in front of her.

If you love a misery addict, perhaps you can see now why she hasn't been able to pull herself out of her situation on her own. Recovering from any addiction is a challenge, but the special characteristics of a misery addiction make the task daunting.

Yet it is a task that is entirely doable. Misery addicts succeed at it daily.

Still, recovery from misery addiction has special requirements. The recovery process can't proceed in a copycat fashion exactly like recovery from other addictions. In recovering from an addiction to misery, attention to the deeper issues and skill training must be present nearly from the beginning. This is an addiction so entwined with disorder and dilemma that recovery must occur hand in hand with therapy and structure.

CHAPTER SIX

Yes or No?

Tonya loved the Seattle Men's Chorus Christmas concert. For her it kicked off the holiday season each year. There was never any question in her mind that she and her best friend would go.

Yet every year, when the announcement came in the mail, she'd put off reserving her seat. One year she waited so late that no seats were available. She missed it and mourned it. The next year, when the announcement came, she _____. (You fill in the blank. Your clue: Tonya is a misery addict.)*

Sanderson hoped to be picked to head up the new software project. He knew he'd increase his chances if he took a course in the new programming language. He had the money. He had the time. He kept waffling about whether or not to take the course.

Elise would be leaving her job soon. Her insurance coverage would end one month after she walked out the door. She needed carpal tunnel surgery. She had the sick leave required and her work could be covered by her colleagues. She couldn't decide whether to do it or not.

Elise, Sanderson, and Tonya all received notices that a program for misery addiction was being held in their city. As each of them read the flyer, lights went on in their heads. Suddenly they had an

*Answer: Tonya put off making a reservation until only nosebleed singles were available.

explanation for why they kept messing up their own lives. They took the little test on the back of the flyer and realized this program was exactly what they needed, designed for a condition they hadn't even realized they had.

They couldn't decide whether to sign up for it or not.

Elise took the problem to her best friend. She sat in Akua's kitchen and said, "I don't know what to do."

"About the surgery?"

"I don't know what to do about that either."

Akua plunked teacups onto the table and sat opposite her friend. "Elise, I don't get it. You need the surgery. You have the insurance now. If you wait till later, it'll only get worse, you risk damage to your nerves, and you will have to pay for it yourself."

"Read this flyer. It fits me to a T."

Akua scanned it and tossed it on the table. "It's you, girl. Makes more sense than anything I've ever seen. Have you sent in your money?"

"I can't decide whether to do it."

"What's to decide? This explains a condition that has kept you stuck your whole life. Now here's a way out of it going on right here in town."

"It's months long."

"So put off your trip. Besides, what's months compared to the years you've lost following your tail in a circle?"

"I don't know. Maybe I'll do it next year."

Akua blew out a breath of air and shook her head. "You don't even know if it'll be offered here next year. Maybe next year it's in Timbuktu and airfare would cost a mint. Besides which, you don't like to fly. Timing's perfect, and you'd miss it?"

Elise shrugged.

Akua tried once more to hold on to her calm. "It seems so logical to me. You have a problem. The answer is right in front of you. The cost for accepting the answer is a whole lot cheaper in time, health, and money than rejecting the answer. This is true whether we're talking about the program or the surgery."

"I can't decide," said Elise plaintively. "I don't know what to do."

Akua jumped to her feet and strode from the kitchen. "I can't stand this. I'm going shopping."

In this brief conversation, two things happened: Elise showed a classic symptom of misery addiction, and Akua absorbed Elise's conflicted energy and couldn't tolerate it.

Perhaps the most difficult thing about being a friend of a misery addict is watching the indecision. It's understandable that it takes a while to make a decision when a choice has equal amounts of good and bad, or if two perfectly desirable options are in conflict. What's more difficult to comprehend is indecision around an option that has mostly an upside—especially if saying no has mostly a downside.

If we could travel back to Elise's childhood, we'd see scenes like this:

"Elise, what do you have on? You look ugly in that shirt. I don't know why you insist on wearing so much blue. Wear pink. Little girls wear pink."

"I don't like pink. I like blue."

"Blue is stupid. Blue is for boys. You will wear pink."

"Why do you hang out with her? She's from the wrong side of town."

"All you do is ski. I want you home on Saturdays."

"No, you can't take a music class. No, you can't play the flute. No, you can't join marching band. These won't put food on your table when you grow up."

"What do you mean you didn't know that? Everyone knows that."

"That can't be your major in college—not if you want us to pay for it."

Most misery addicts endured childhoods crammed with criticism and harsh judgment. Most were systematically separated from their own impulses, preferences, feelings, likes, and interests. Most were pressured to move toward their dislikes, which were often a parent's or family's likes.

As children, misery addicts had natural preferences that typically led to disdain, ridicule, or punishment. Thus it was a lot safer to conform and make themselves do, eat, wear, or study the things they weren't drawn to. They learned to move toward the things they weren't drawn to and to avoid the things they preferred. Their wires got crossed.

Look at this definition of memory, from *The Developing Mind* by Daniel Siegel:

> Memory is more than what we can consciously recall about events from the past. A broader definition is that *memory is the way past events affect future function.* Memory is thus the way the brain is affected by experience and then subsequently alters its future responses. In this view, the brain experiences the world and encodes this interaction in a manner that alters future ways of responding. . . . past events can directly shape how and what we learn, even though we may have no conscious recollection of those events. Our earliest experiences shape our ways of behaving, including patterns of relating to others, without our ability to recall consciously when these first learning experiences occurred.[1]

Siegel then describes the mental encoding process, which involves a neural net that creates a particular firing pattern throughout the brain.

> If a certain pattern has been stimulated in the past, the probability of activating a similar profile in the future is enhanced. If the pattern is fired repeatedly, the probability of future activation is further increased. The increased probability is created by changes in the synaptic connections within the network of neurons.[2]

A synapse is the gap that occurs between the end of one nerve fiber and the beginning of the next one. Infants are born with lots of neurons and relatively few synapses. The placement and creation of a synapse is determined by an individual's experience and genetic information.[3]

It turns out that the physical structure of the brain is unique to each person and is a result of experiences.[4] Changes in synaptic connections alter the ways in which the brain functions.[5] Then these alterations influence a person's subsequent behavior, perceptions, and thoughts.

An easy way to remember this is Hebb's axiom: "Neurons that fire together wire together."[6]

Once a brain is wired in a certain pattern, it can create automatic behavior. Elise demonstrated this in her indecision. As a child she was criticized for virtually everything that originated from her own inner self—her taste in clothing, her choice of friends, even her food preferences. She wasn't just encouraged to toe the family line. She was punished if she didn't.

She became a product of classical conditioning. She was rewarded with safety and inclusion if she did just what her parents wanted. She was punished anytime she followed her own heart.

How then, as an adult, could she be expected to honor her heart? When she had an interest or a preference, she was a deer in the headlights. She froze. She could not make herself take a step toward something that in the past had always netted pain. She could only safely choose options that didn't appeal to her.

Tonya's pain and punishment were of a different variety, but they resulted in a similar pattern. Tonya was the child who wasn't liked. Two girls and a boy were born in that family. The boy was treated like a prince; the other daughter was fawned over and protected. Tonya, for some reason, was not what the family was looking for when they had another child. Emotionally, they dropped her.

She tried all sorts of ways of getting in. Some worked; some didn't. By the age of six, she had figured out that if she served the other members of her family, did things for them, and immediately let go of any interest of hers that fell outside the family line, they sort of included her. Otherwise, she was wallpaper.

This made her afraid of her own interests. It also made her fear expulsion if she did something she wanted to do.

REJECTED CHILDREN

Not a lot is said about an unfavored child, but I find a high proportion of them among misery addicts. Sometimes the dislike is subtle, demonstrated through preferential behavior toward other children. Sometimes it's stated outright, with comparative statements that designate one child as treasure and the other as trinket.

A favored child's behavior tends to be interpreted in a positive light. He's talked of glowingly and given favors and privileges. The rejected child is given dregs, hounded, compared negatively to others, or handled irritably and impatiently. His behavior is cast as selfish, mean, lazy, or stupid.

Growing up, Tonya's sister was held up as an example. "Why can't you be more like Cliona?" "There's no point taking *you* shopping. Cliona needs a new dress, so she and I will go by ourselves."

Even though she was the younger child, Tonya was expected to perform at the older child's level. "She can sit still. Why can't you?"

Tonya was expected to know what the older child had been taught, even though Tonya hadn't been shown. "Tonya, I left you a note to light the oven when you got home from school."

"I didn't know how, Mom. I was scared it would blow up."

"That's silly. It won't blow up if you do it right."

"I don't know how to do it."

"Of course you do. We light the oven all the time."

"You've never shown me."

"You were just too lazy to pull your nose out of a book and watch."

In some families, abuse is laughed off. A brother is favored over the sister so that when he hits her or stands on her hair—or when he terrorizes her or molests her—the parents brush it aside. In Tonya's case, a sister was favored. When Cliona ruined Tonya's clothes, said nasty things, or left Tonya in dangerous situations, it was not taken seriously by their parents.

Sometimes a child is rejected because the parents didn't want to become parents. Sanderson was resented by his parents because he was the reason they had to get married. His mother hadn't wanted to be pregnant, didn't like being pregnant, and didn't like dealing with Sanderson's bodily needs when he was a baby. It was a bad start for this mother-son relationship that neither ever got over.

His mother was always standoffish with him. His father was distant. They never realized that they were dumping issues onto him that were theirs alone to deal with.

Later children were exempt because by then the marriage was a fact.

Sanderson felt the rejection for thirty years before he began to understand what it was about. That was way too late to save his self-esteem. At an early age he believed himself to be a person who would be resented and rejected.

A baby is never responsible for being born; the parents caused that to happen. Yet an amazing number of children are resented and rejected because they are seen as the reason a parent got trapped.

Sometimes a mother will reject a daughter because of her body. A thin, possibly anorexic mother with her own phobia about fat may perceive her daughter's natural pudginess and bone structure as a weight problem and ride her mercilessly about her eating and her body. A large mother, hating her own body, may reject the daughter whose body type is similar. Either situation can cause a child to hate and mistrust her body and lead to an eating disorder.

A child will feel even more hopeless if there's a "perfect" sibling who gets all the attention and compliments. "Look at what your sister is eating. She's happy with that lettuce leaf and radish." "I'd get clothes for you too, if you lost twenty pounds."

When a child hates her body, it doesn't stop at the skin. Her dislike for herself spreads out into wariness of her thoughts and ideas and into distrust of her own interests and instincts.

Parental neglect can also be passive—not deliberately directed at a particular child and not due to a conflict in personalities, but the result of some other situation in the parent's life. In comparison to the other siblings, one child may thus seem neglected or singled out.

In some cases, parents may have unknowingly used themselves up before their last child is born. At this point they have no more energy for guiding a child, listening to babble, or going to PTA meetings. Other common possibilities: One child can be sick for an extended time, and a parent's time is taken up in nursing duties leaving no energy for the other child. A financial crisis may direct parental attention to long working hours. Parental addiction or illness may eliminate one parent from the scene and siphon energy and attention from the other.

When all children in a family are treated meanly and harshly, it's damaging, of course. But if one child is singled out for rejection or is the lone recipient of neglect, it feels more personal. It puts that one child on the outside and seeds the belief that she is irredeemably different, destined for separateness, unlovable at a cellular level.

Unfortunately, it's easy in such situations to cross a child's emotional wiring and turn him against himself. These crossed wires often lead to an adult who has difficulty making choices for his own benefit.

CHAPTER SEVEN

Don't Push Me

Elise survived her family by sheer grit. When her father was beating her, she reached down to a stubborn place inside and said to herself, "He won't defeat me. I won't cry. I won't show pain."

As an adult, Elise froze when she was in doubt, and nothing could move her out of it for as long as she remained unsure.

Since she was often not sure, she was often immobilized.

What would have happened if Akua, in her kitchen, had pushed Elise to decide then and there about the surgery or had insisted that she sign up for the recovery program? What if Akua had dialed the surgeon's office and put Elise in a position where she'd have to schedule the surgery?

She'd have moved into the sequel to indecision—resistance. Push a misery addict too hard and the chances are she will do exactly the opposite of what is best for her. If Akua had forced Elise to schedule the surgery, she'd probably have cancelled it as soon as Akua was gone. (Notice that it's far easier to stop a good thing than it is to start it.)

A new, more compelling incentive would take over—the absolute need to not be controlled. It would matter more to Elise to not be controlled than to lose the use of her hand.

Not all misery addicts were overcontrolled as children—some suffered from too little structure—but those who were have a fierce aversion to restriction, so much so that they must buck it even if the consequences will harm them.

Sanderson was fortunate to work at a job with flextime. As long as he worked his eight hours, he could start and stop whenever he wanted. He never abused this; in fact, he often gave the company extra minutes here and there. However, he *was* expected to meet report deadlines and to turn in paperwork at specific times. This he could not do.

He'd program his computer with alarms. He put notes to himself in his Palm Pilot. None of it worked. After he received some serious warnings, he created a predeadline with a buddy at which time he was to produce his reports. But even then, he always had something else to do first. He always had an excuse. His paperwork was still always late.

This behavior didn't get him fired (although it could have), but it did cost him. His supervisors came to view him as resistant, insubordinate, disorganized, and not dedicated to his job. In fact, he loved his job. But his behavior gave an opposite impression.

Tonya kept trying to lose weight. After running the gamut of weight-loss programs and losing a total of three pounds, she finally found a binge-eating recovery group that revealed to her the true nature of the problem. There, she learned about the importance of always having breakfast and never skipping meals. With help she created a plan for herself and set up daily phone support with a group member. But within weeks she bailed out of her plan.

Tonya and Sanderson survived their families by constructing an inner barrier that made it possible to endure eighteen years of arbitrary, mean-spirited domination. As a result, they experienced nearly any kind of structure in adulthood as unbearable. Discipline felt like regimentation. Supervision felt like bossiness. To comply with authority felt like servitude.

This kind of problem can spread out so that any program or activity that requires consistency triggers rebellion. A daily exercise program, a routine for house maintenance, a school study schedule, or a wife's request for a Friday date night can slip into that haunt that must be avoided, regardless of the cost.

Unfortunately, though, life is filled with routines—daily hygiene, meals, dental checkups, cleaning the aquarium, filling the bird feeder, changing the car oil, having annual physicals, taking vitamins and medications, and going to recovery meetings.

A misery addict's paralysis is enhanced by this aversion to control. Any pressure, however well meant or kindly, will be resisted. If the pressure increases, at some level, most misery addicts will rebel. This creates a life that's unmanageable.

This looks, from the outside, like the misery addict is choosing to be miserable. It's more accurate to say that she cannot let herself feel trapped.

MEMORY REVISITED

Let's look at memory again. There are two kinds of memory: explicit and implicit. Explicit memory is what we use to store and retrieve facts. The multiplication tables, phone numbers, our past experiences, and a sense of self all involve explicit memory.

The encoding process of explicit memory goes through stages: short-term memory, working memory, and, eventually, long-term memory. Full encoding (consolidation into permanent memory) can take weeks, months, even years. The parts of the brain involved in encoding develop throughout childhood.[1]

Certain conditions must be met if facts are to be stored and used. For example, the person must be conscious. His attention must be directed and focused if something is to be remembered.

Implicit memory is already working at birth. It involves parts of the brain that do not require conscious processing, parts that are intact at birth and remain intact throughout life. Implicit memory works through mental models generated from the neural net. Instead of going through stages that can take weeks or months before a fact is in hard storage, implicit memory records our full experience, including our sensations, how we feel about them, and the markers that identify them. Remarkably, from birth, infants are able to generalize from experience and do so beyond the single mode of the experience. From feeling a nipple in their mouths in a darkened room, they can identify the familiar nipple in a visual multiple choice. They have generalized from touch to vision.[2] Already, in early life, a baby's brain has developed shorthand for recognition. Her brain is capable of recognizing what is familiar and of having a bias toward it.

In fact, she can *anticipate* what will come next based on previous experience and react in advance. Thus a baby can cry at the smell of the doctor's office where he previously had a shot or be restless in church where he previously got too hungry.

Anticipating the future is a product of *implicit* memory. In contrast, planning for the future is a function of *explicit* memory.[3]

How often are we caught short by expectations? After an event, we realize it has failed or exceeded our expectations, but prior to an event, unless we are somehow stimulated to talk about it, we aren't aware of our expectations. Expectations arise from anticipation, and anticipation is based on implicit memory.

This points out an essential difference between implicit and explicit memory. With explicit memory, we are *aware* that we are remembering. We can feel ourselves remembering. We are looking into our brains to get information.

With implicit memory, we have no sense of recollection. We have no subjective experience of remembrance. We are not aware that our thoughts, feelings, and perceptions are being influenced by implicit memory because we do not feel ourselves remembering. Thus we are not conscious of the generalizations we are making or of how we are slotting current experience into pigeonholes formed by past experience.

It is implicit memory that creates the detrimental reflexes that mess up a misery addict's life. But because he has no sensation of remembering, he does not know he's being influenced. These behaviors and reactions feel natural and automatic, and the misery addict may sometimes be surprised if they are pointed out afterward because they can be so mechanical that the person is not even aware that he has acted. He may be particularly unaware of *why* he has acted.

Misery addicts get puzzled by their own behavior. Sanderson will be heading to a recovery meeting and end up at the software store. Tonya will be determined to order salad and end up with a burger and fries. Why? Because their behavior is overruled by a deeper impulse, one coming from a place deeper than consciousness.

When we realize that these impulses were formed during baby-hood, it makes a little more sense that we can't remember them. But it can be very disorienting when a self-destructive behavior sneaks up on us, especially when we're intentionally trying to be conscious and keep ourselves from sabotaging ourselves.

The irony is that a misery addict who hates being controlled is, in fact, constantly being driven by implicit memory.

This is true for all of us, of course, but if our wires aren't crossed, it's not necessarily a problem. If things that are good for us seem positive and things harmful to us seem negative, we can navigate the world with some confidence.

For the misery addict, implicit memory colors her reaction to positive possibilities and choices. The things that are good for her have a bad feel. Thus her instinct tells her to follow the road that will not be best for her. Her bias is toward the familiar, and what is familiar is her system of survival.

Friends and family members may see a misery addict as wantonly self-destructive and may decide to bail out of the relationship. Sometimes the only sane choice for a friend or family member is to do so. A misery addict's behavior *can* be self-destructive—and, even if it's not deliberate, loved ones get tired of being helpless in the face of the misery addict's dedication to a collision course. Sometimes, by the time he's willing to go into recovery and treatment, he's used up the people who cared about him the most.

Therapists may judge such a client as oppositional, and their commitment to the client may erode. (Ordinary therapy alone can't fix this anyway, unless it's a mild case. In most cases it must be coupled with recovery, and it must include certain other elements, which you'll learn about soon.)

One spring day I was walking near my office when I noticed a little curly-headed girl walking in her play yard just as her father came around the corner of the house and through the gate. The child had a toy in her hand, and when she saw her father, she held the toy forward, as if offering it. In response, her father harshly barked a rejecting stream of words.

The child did an abrupt about-face, slumped, dropped the toy, and walked away from him, dejection writ throughout her small body.

Imagine the affect on her neural net, the immediate associations engraved in the indelible material of her brain. Imagine what she was learning to anticipate about men, about adults, about close relatives.

A new child absorbs the world at an astounding rate. These early models become her slant on life, her beliefs about the way relationships work.

Here is the dilemma for misery addicts: what do you do when the actions you need to take to save your life are the very actions that feel most life-threatening?

CHAPTER EIGHT

Isolation and Pseudo-Intimacy

The little curly-headed child stayed in my mind. I replayed the look on her face when she saw her father. She didn't smile—a natural response in a toddler seeing a loving parent after a separation. She held that toy out, as if she was used to this man taking things from her and she was going to give it up quickly. She wasn't more than three years old and had already learned to fear him.

He barked at her. Her effort to protect herself—by giving up the toy—failed.

If events continue in this sequence, this child will learn that she can't influence, can't predict, and can't stop negative responses from this man. If her mother also fears him and doesn't stop him, the child will generalize and anticipate this experience in intimate relationships.

It is unlikely that these events would be stored in explicit memory. Her brain was too young to record this incident as factual. The whole of the experience would be stored in implicit memory, influencing her view of intimacy, yet she would not be able to recall it.

The experiences we can't recall aren't real to us. We can't use them to explain attitudes or fears or persistent reactions that cause us unhappiness—yet they permeate our perceptions and create our biases.

They influence us powerfully, but, because we can't recall them, we can't talk about them. And, since we can't talk about them, we can't defuse them the way we can soothe traumatic events that we remember.

Thus our repertoire for intimacy is set by a host of experiences we can't remember.

Yet we need intimacy. We need close connection with others. Failing that, we have to connect to something.

Any aspects of our environment that we associate in our implicit memory with connection will give us the experience of connection in adulthood.

For example, I love to do laundry. I feel safe and joyful when I hang laundry on a line. For years I didn't question this. Recently, though, I recalled mornings spent with my beloved grandmother while she hung laundry on a line. The smell of freshly washed sheets, the sound of them flapping in a breeze, the sight of sheets strung in a row—all this gives me comfort. It is associated with my connection with my dear grandmother.

Conversely, things we associate with pain and disconnection will give us unpleasant feelings in adulthood.

When she grows up, the little curly-headed girl might associate fear and rejection with toys, yards, grass, spring, men, giving, or seeing someone unexpectedly. Who knows what aspect of that harsh encounter will stay embedded in her for a lifetime, creating an unexplainable aversion.

Last November, Bridie joined a women's exercise club in which the machines were set in a circle. Women joined the circuit at any point and shifted to the next station every half minute in response to recorded instructions. It was the first program she'd ever been able to stay with. She raved about it to Dara, her sister, who then joined the same program in another city.

Each night, faithfully, Bridie stopped at the club on the way home from work. Then in April, a weird thing happened. Moments after she leaned back into a certain machine, her heart began pounding and her eyes blurred. She fainted. The club staff called an ambulance and monitored her, fearing a heart attack.

At the hospital, the symptoms went away, and she was released without need of further treatment.

The next day, as she opened the door of the club, a great fear seized her and she couldn't go in.

Soon after, Dara came to visit. She wanted to go to the club and was surprised that Bridie didn't want to go with her. Bridie said, "I can't. I can't even walk in there anymore." She explained about her attack.

Mystified, Dara went into the club. She did the circuit and then one of the machines caused her to lean back putting the skylight in her view; beneath the skylight rotated a ceiling fan. In a flash of insight she had the answer.

When Bridie was almost four years old and Dara was eight, they lived in an isolated part of Canada. One day their mother collapsed. The whole family and most of the neighborhood stood outside on a summer afternoon when a helicopter came and took her away. She died; they never saw her again.

It was devastating for Dara, but the whole family figured that Bridie wasn't much affected, being too young to remember.

Throughout the darkness of winter, no light shone through that skylight when Bridie stopped after work. In April, though, after daylight saving time began, Bridie saw a blade beating in a circle against a bright sky, just like the helicopter that stole her mother.

Implicit memory creates associations that then influence our feelings, thoughts, and actions.

When Kali Rose was a little girl, her father came back from the Korean War. He came back angry. Kali Rose was abandoned instantly as her mother focused all of her attention and energy on him. From then on Kali Rose was a lonely child floating in a household with a perpetually angry and dissatisfied man and a scared, dependent mother. Two years old is way too early to lose a mother, even if she stays in the house. Plus, her mother was the only person Kali Rose had bonded to. When her mother dropped her end of the relationship, it spelled catastrophe for Kali Rose.

When Kali Rose was forced toward her father, with his red face and his furious energy, she'd push away. This made him angrier. He was not going to let a two-year-old tell him what to do, so he would then force closeness.

Powerful associations were captured in Kali Rose's implicit memory, yet she cannot recall any of it. She doesn't understand herself when she is completely uninterested in people who pursue her but falls deeply in love with people who can't offer her connection.

Kali Rose has experienced a certain excruciating vignette over and over. Here is one example. She was producing an art show and had invited her friends to come see it. She wanted them to see something she was good at; she wanted to share the achievement. One friend, Jhone, came, loved the show, and said so. Jhone then got lost in the paintings and, in a haze of art bliss, left.

Kali Rose, penetratingly perceptive (as most misery addicts are), felt the shift of energy in the room as soon as Jhone was gone. She was inconsolable at first. Then she became furious. Later they talked, and no matter what Jhone said, Kali Rose could not let go of one point: "How could you leave without telling me good-bye?"

It took months for Kali Rose to get over this. It was impossible for her to make room in herself for her friend's reality—which was that the show was so powerful that Jhone floated to the ozone and lost contact with the earth.

Kali Rose could have gotten a positive message from this, which was that her work was stunning, mind-blowing. But Kali Rose could focus on only one thing—that she was abruptly abandoned.

We can see clearly the connection between Kali Rose's reaction to Jhone and her experience of her mother's abrupt emotional departure—"without even saying good-bye"—translated as leaving without warning, leaving without preparation.

Kali Rose aches when someone turns her back, when someone she cares about puts all her attention on someone else. First she hurts, and then she gets furious.

Anything that looks like abrupt abandonment, however innocent or unintentional on the other's part, sends this sequence of hurt and outrage coursing through her.

Jhone, caring deeply about Kali Rose, decided to become intentional whenever departing from her. (Sometimes friends will make such an accommodation out of love and an acceptance of their friends' issues.)

However, if Kali Rose persists in being able to hold only her own reality when conflicts happen and is unable to see that a friend's actions can be innocent, she will lose friends and intimates.

And this will replay her childhood experience.

This is the devastating cycle for misery addicts. They long for connection. They yearn for intimacy. But as someone gets closer, he eventually, unknowingly, triggers an association embedded so deeply in their hearts that they don't even know where it comes from.

Then they have what looks like an extreme reaction. (It is extreme for the current situation but probably fits the unrecalled childhood situation.) Thus they appear to be shooting themselves in the foot because the potential intimate starts backing off.

And then they're alone again.

One way misery addicts resolve this paradox is by being attracted to people who can't offer intimacy. Another is by connecting with activities or situations that feel like family.

A service provided by addiction is that it gives us connection. We feel connected to the bottle or the food, to the gym or the casino. Like-minded people in those places can become pseudo-family, "where everybody knows your name." The pseudo-family members won't turn controlling because they aren't that invested in us. Yet we feel like we belong because, as that situation becomes more and more familiar, we learn how to operate well within it.

Addiction and pseudo-intimacies are ways out of isolation.

ISOLATION

Many misery addicts are wonderful friends, and many have some wonderful friends, but letting even their closest friend close is difficult. The isolation experienced by a misery addict is terrible and profound. It is deeper than a well and darker than a cave.

Every single misery addict I've worked with longs for intimacy the way we long for breath. Yet they set themselves up to miss intimacy by filling their spaces with people who don't have it to give, people who are emotionally unavailable, and people with whom intimacy would be a boundary violation, such as therapists and ministers.

They've been hurt so deeply in the past that they can't get themselves to risk another try at true intimacy. Their despair and hopelessness, their belief that they'll never get to have what they want, prevents them from putting themselves into situations that would expose them to people who could offer intimacy.

Even when intimacy is staring them in the face, they may unknowingly turn a potential connection away. Intimacy is longed for and feared, wanted and avoided. Intimacy is both delicious and terrifying.

It's hard for misery addicts to understand that intimacy is a skill like most other things, something that can be learned and developed, like exercising a toe muscle. They are more likely to see intimacy as a prize that is bestowed to people a lot less deserving than themselves, a medal that is somehow given to people who should have received just honorable mentions.

Even with good, trustworthy friends, they are more likely to give than receive, to conceal their deepest feelings and thoughts. They may have trouble asking for help or put on a happy, resilient, or uncaring charade.

Ingrid, who had a brilliant mind, protected herself from disappointment by never asking for what she wanted. During Ingrid's childhood, when she and her siblings made their Christmas lists and hung them on the fridge, Ingrid's list bore no resemblance to her true desires. Then, when her family overruled her choices, it didn't hurt. She didn't get what she didn't want. Of course, she didn't get what she did want either. But she had come up with a way to make the hurt less personal. If she didn't ask, she couldn't be hurt when they didn't do it.

Unfortunately, this system has evolved into a way of life for the adult Ingrid. She still doesn't ask. Half the time, she doesn't know what she wants. She decorates her house based on what an imaginary mate might like. She goes to the restaurant *you* like. Her friendships are based on what she does for others. Her parties center around her friends' interests.

As you can guess, this sets up a system by which her friends disregard her. She's invisible to them. They think she's a mirror. On the rare occasion she really wants to do something, her friends cancel. They aren't used to directing their attention to her, so they don't take her few requests seriously.

She is surrounded by a group of people who treat her exactly the way her family treated her. The center of the party, Ingrid is unbearably lonely.

Two things are needed for intimacy: astute judgment about who can connect and the skills that nurture connection. Misery addicts often have neither.

A host of behaviors can work *against* intimacy. Many of these are the routine repertoire of a misery addict.

Both of Paloma's parents were critical. Her father's abusiveness came from anger. Her mother's hurtful comments arose from fear. Anger is intrusive, but fear is quiet; so, between the two parents, Paloma turned more to her mother.

She loved her mother deeply, and her way of entering intimacy with her was to experience her feelings for her. Her mother had lost a lot in her life, but she never grieved it. Paloma grieved on her mother's behalf, over and over.

When anger was ruling Paloma's father—which was most of the time—he acted in ways that were abusive. For example, when Paloma was slow to eat a vegetable she didn't like, he dumped the bowl of vegetables on her head.

Paloma had a slight margin of safety when her mother was around. Her mother didn't stop her husband from his abuse, but she would sometimes offer Paloma comfort afterward.

One week, Paloma was left home while her mother went to a distant city to tend a sick relative. Paloma doesn't remember what happened during that week, but something terrible did, something involving her father.

We don't know what her father was capable of when no one but Paloma was witnessing him. We can only excavate possibilities from the associations Paloma carries now. Here are the artifacts:

- When the possibility of true intimacy is offered Paloma, she gets sick.
- She has a powerful aversion to being close to someone she loves.

- When someone she loves offers connection, her thoughts get intensely focused on someone who has no commitment to her, someone who is obsessed with someone else.
- She hates to be home. When she is home, she loses all her energy.
- She has a lot of shame about her body.

While we can't know the specifics, it's clear that, during her childhood, someone she loved hurt her terribly, that this happened in her home, and that an indelible link formed between being close to a loved one and being terribly hurt.

Today, as an adult, she protects herself by aborting intimate moments and curtailing intimate opportunities, and her body helps her stay away from these opportunities through sickness.

Intimacy involves risk. Sometimes the risk doesn't work out. When that happens, we have to be able to survive it. We have to be able to pick ourselves up and go on.

For a misery addict, the risk is usually too great. Implicit memory expects intimacy to cause devastation, precisely because *failed* intimacy is perceived as life-threatening. So the misery addict simply wards off intimacy time after time.

CHAPTER NINE

Sacrifice and the System

"Ingrid, you haven't swept behind the table."

Ingrid glanced at her older sister, then maneuvered the broom, which was taller than she was, behind the kitchen table. "I can't get it all the way back here. The table is too close to the wall."

Her much-older sister Anja was sitting at the table, sucking on sugar cubes. "We wouldn't have such a small kitchen if you'd been a boy. You were supposed to be a boy. You could have roomed with Jake, and then we wouldn't have had to move into this house with its little cramped rooms. It's your fault we live in this house."

Ingrid's face crumpled. She glanced at her sister with hurt eyes.

"Mom said I have to take you with me today because they'll all be working. I'm going to Jordan's house. You'd better stay quiet and sit in the corner and not do any dumb sister thing or I'll make you go outside in the rain by yourself."

"I'm hungry."

"You can have some crackers. You don't get lunch because you're too fat. The whole reason Mom and Dad have to work on Saturday is because they have to buy you clothes. You were supposed to wear what I wore and what Lavren wore before me. But you're so fat they have to *buy* you clothes. So they have to work, and I'm stuck with you."

Ingrid, not fat but with a larger bone structure than her sisters, finished pushing the dirt into the dustpan and emptied the pan. She kept her eyes lowered so that Anja wouldn't see her tears.

"Now you're going to cry, aren't you, crybaby? Maybe I'll just leave you alone in the house all day."

"No!" Ingrid cried out. She was scared in the house alone.

"Okay, then promise you won't say anything at Jordan's house. You stay in the corner and don't ask for anything."

"I promise."

Such moments were permanently etched in Ingrid's memory. Many years later, as an adult, she was still controlled by these early events, but unconsciously.

Ingrid slapped shut the patient's chart and slotted it into the holder. She glanced over at Jasmine, stooping to get her purse out of the drawer inside the nurses' station. "You want to do a pay-check party tonight?"

"Sure."

Ingrid stood up and stretched her back. She could feel her extra pounds after a day of maneuvering orthopedic patients. "Where do you want to go?"

"Do you have anything in mind?"

Ingrid thought about her favorite group, playing this week at the Jazz Alley. "I don't care."

"Well, then let's just go to Red Robin like we always do."

"Okay, I'll round up the others." Ingrid pushed the chair under the counter. "I can drive."

"I'm so glad you drive all the time. I hate driving."

Me too, thought Ingrid.

As they waited for their meals, Ingrid sighed and said, "I don't want to go home tonight."

The other women looked at her in surprise. They weren't used to Ingrid initiating a comment about herself. It was as if a chair had spoken.

"Why not?" asked Jasmine.

"Oh, I've been letting this woman stay with me because she's been sick and unable to work, and now I don't like being home so much."

"You don't like her?" asked Chelly.

"She's okay, but she has two yippy dogs that she won't keep off the furniture no matter how many times I ask, and when I get home, she follows me around. I can't get away from her."

Jasmine leaned back in her chair. "How much rent is she paying?"

Ingrid gave Jasmine a sheepish look. "Nothing."

"How long has she been staying with you?"

Ingrid looked down as if ashamed. "Ten months."

"Ten months?" Jasmine made a face. "Is she a relative?"

"No."

"Is she a *girl* friend?" asked Chelly.

Ingrid understood the reference. "No. The truth is, I don't even like her."

"How do you know her?"

"She's in my book club."

"What does she do in return—you know, to balance what you do for her?" asked Jasmine.

"She eats the food I've set aside for my healthy food plan. She brings sugary foods into the house, which I'm trying to stay abstinent from. She stands and prattles at me, in *my* bathroom, while I'm brushing my teeth."

"She's in your face while you're brushing your teeth?" Jasmine wailed. "Girl, you need some help with your 'no' skills."

"I'll go home with you," volunteered Chelly, "and walk up to her and say, 'Can you spell *privacy*?'"

"Can you spell *boundary*?" laughed Ingrid.

"Can you spell *Get the hell out and take those yappy things with you*?"

As we learned earlier, Ingrid wasn't reared by her parents. Her resentful sister played mother to Ingrid. From Anja she got her self-image, her life charter, and her instruction about how to be with others. She grew up feeling in the way, a tagalong, the one who caused others hardship because she was the wrong gender and the wrong size. She got to be included only by doing all the work, not asking for anything, and not saying much.

When her sister got mad at her, she left Ingrid in the house alone. Ingrid associated being alone with being punished. She spent many dark nights alone and terrified. As an adult, she alternates some tense months trying to enjoy living by herself with a series of uncooperative or narcissistic roommates. Her fear of aloneness causes her to fill her life with people, and her habit of hiding from herself causes her to pick people who are takers.

She gravitates toward people who, like her sister, aren't invested in her. As she did for her sister, she does chores for them and helps them keep their lives running, while hers is put on a shelf.

Ingrid is a misery addict by default. She doesn't choose to be miserable. But her training had such an impact on her that she doesn't know how to get out of the box. In general, she feels wrong—for her size, her style, her interests. She's made herself as beige as possible, doesn't say too much about what she wants, tends to be the one to make events work.

Like most misery addicts, she's stuck in her system of survival. She's miserable as a consequence of running her life by her system.

Ingrid's sabotage is subtle. She hurts herself by not choosing. She goes along. She finds friends who appreciate her services, who are unconcerned about returning favors, and who use her. These folks fill time for her; then she goes home sad at not being known and dulls the sadness through TV and snacking.

Sometimes a person will try to reciprocate with Ingrid. Chelly would have been Ingrid's friend, a closer friend than just an acquaintance at paycheck dinners. She tried to return favors, but Ingrid wouldn't let her. She tried to offer to drive, but Ingrid insisted. Chelly asked questions about Ingrid's life only to have Ingrid divert the conversation back to Chelly.

Chelly backed off because she couldn't wrestle the relationship onto balanced ground. Ingrid was insistent on staying in her pattern. Chelly soon realized she couldn't budge it. She gave up, and Ingrid never saw that she'd lost an opportunity for a healthy friend.

In this way, she screened her friends. The self-centered ones found a good deal. The conscious, reciprocating ones left.

Ingrid's life reveals another aspect of a misery addict's allegiance to her system of survival. It's unyielding. It's impervious. And to a large extent, it's unconscious.

When Ingrid was made conscious of her system—the strength of it, the comprehensiveness of it, and the consequences of it on her lifestyle—she could begin to see it, but she didn't have any idea how to act differently. Her system held her like nylon net. Stepping outside it was very scary.

A system founded in fear can only be renovated in safety. Force just causes a person to curl up inside it. It's like the challenge between the wind and the sun. The wind insisted it could blow the coat off the traveler. The sun bet it could do it. The wind blew and blew, and the traveler only pulled his coat tighter around him. The sun's warm rays caused the man to loosen his coat voluntarily.

You can soften your fingernails by soaking them in warm water. In a similar way, it's possible to soften a stuck system by soaking it in the company of warm, safe, intentional people. It also helps to be guided by an expert on relationships and recovery.

Yet a misery addict may get so frightened when she steps outside of her system that, regardless of how miserable it makes her, she'll fight to keep it.

In an attempt at recovery, Ingrid began a healing retreat for misery addiction. Although she did well at the retreat center, Ingrid began sabotaging her gains almost immediately whenever she left the center. Each weekend, instead of spending time in the room she had paid for, with people and a structure that supported her recovery, she went back home and mixed with people who used her.

Though Ingrid wouldn't fight for herself, she did fight for her system. She showed great strength in concealing her involvement in activities that increased her misery and avoidance, in deceiving her therapist, and in setting up inarguable reasons for missing recovery weekends.

So we have the contrast of Ingrid appearing weak while showing great strength in preserving her system. At the center of her relapse, and her pattern, was giving charge of her life to people who use her.

Her treatment friends don't use her. But the people who do use her feel familiar and like home to her, so she fought to keep them. She couldn't keep herself from reenacting her patterns, regardless of their negative consequences and their sabotaging effect on the gains she had made.

Intelligence does not make it easier to drop the system. Remember, Ingrid has a brilliant mind. Yet she holds to her system like glue, resisting positive outcomes tenaciously.

— Exercise 1: Your System —

Each of us lives according to an internal system, one we've developed based on our experiences growing up. Each person's system is a combination of healthy and unhealthy behaviors, thoughts, expectations, and responses. However, some systems are healthier and more realistic than others.

For the next half hour, I'd like you to answer the questions below. First, however, go to a spot that's comfortable, quiet, and free of distractions. If you can't get to such a spot right now, then stop for now and come back to the questions when such a setting is available.

However, please *don't* skip ahead and begin chapter 10 or forget about the questions entirely. They're an important part of getting the most out of this book—and of increasing your own happiness.

When you're ready, take a pen and paper, or sit down in front of your computer. Get comfortable and begin.

1. If something feels scary to you—a job assignment, a friend's reaction—what do you do?
2. In what ways do you protect yourself from feeling afraid?
3. How do you keep from feeling other feelings that are quite uncomfortable?
4. When someone hurts you, what do you do?
5. Look at the people you tend to hang out with. In general, what kind of people are they? Giving? Withholding? Taking? Using? Admirable? Generous? Kind? Mean?
6. How do you handle tough experiences (like breaking up with someone or losing a job or a friend moving away)?
7. When you feel overwhelmed, what do you do?
8. Was either of your parents harsh, mean, abusive, or critical when you were a child?

9. When you were a child, which parent (or parental figure) had the most impact on you in a negative way?

10. When that parent was at his or her worst, how did you survive that? What did you do to keep from being crushed?

11. Do any of the people in your life now act in a way that is similar to that parent? Who?

12. When you think about the methods you used to keep from being crushed and to make it through your childhood, can you see situations in which you use similar methods now? Which situations? Which methods?

13. Which parent (or parental figure) were you closest to?

14. If you get a very sudden disappointment, what do you do?

15. List ten experiences you want very much to have in your lifetime.

16. In making the list above, did you let yourself list the truest things? Or did you hold back? If so, add the items you were afraid to list before.

17. What steps are you taking to bring these desired experiences into your life?

18. What keeps you from pursuing these desires more actively?

19. What situations or experiences would slow or halt your pursuit?

20. If you could have more help, would it be possible to move more directly or quickly toward fulfilling your desires?

21. What needs to happen in order to get that help?

22. How do you make yourself feel better when something upsets you?

23. Describe any resistance you've been feeling as you've answered these questions.

24. If any of the above questions caused your mind to stop or wander, go back and look at that question again. What feeling or reaction was triggered by that question?

25. What are you feeling right now?

26. Does that feeling remind you of a feeling or experience from when you were growing up? What is it?

SACRIFICE

Many misery addicts are sacrificers. Their system includes sacrificing themselves in various ways for people, ideas, or rules. For example, Ingrid had quite a comprehensive system of self-sacrifice: she gave up her time, interests, ideas, home, money, and preferences for others.

Jules's brand of sacrifice was different. She put all of her effort into pleasing others by doing things for them. A *Good Housekeeping* poster mom, she made her own mayonnaise, drove on all the school outings, vacuumed every day, and sewed Halloween costumes. She was a great mom. Almost. The only thing she didn't teach her children was to have regard for her. They followed their father's lead by expecting her services and being angry if they weren't provided.

When she tried to pursue an interest of her own, even after the kids were grown and gone, she was rebuked by her husband, who then roped in their adult children to side with him and put pressure on her. It was safer for her to keep her attention on others. She was so focused on others that she had disappeared.

Kali Rose also had an external focus. She, too, sacrificed, but her focus was very specific. Her focus was on her mother and any mother stand-in. At every period in her adult life, she had at least one female in an authority position from whom she longed to receive approval. She reacted to every situation in terms of her beliefs about what this esteemed authority was thinking about her. Sometimes that person was a boss, sometimes a therapist, sometimes a friend that Kali Rose had secretly promoted to mentor.

Kali Rose's focus was always on whether she was pleasing or displeasing this woman. Her implicit memory was packed with associations of being rejected by Mom, so she projected disapproval onto these women. She lived in frequent despair that her latest action (or nonaction) had destroyed that woman's regard for her. Then she would do some seriously self-sabotaging thing to punish herself for her (imaginary) mistake.

Most of the time, her projection was false, based on some incident or comment so minor that the woman hadn't even noticed it. What did get the woman's attention, however, was the inexplicable and jarring behavior exhibited by Kali Rose when she was punishing herself.

I've yet to meet a misery addict who doesn't sacrifice herself in some significant way for someone or something else. Sacrifice is a part of the survival system and part of how misery addicts sabotage themselves.

The essence of misery addiction is this war between self-actualization and self-denial. Since many misery addicts have little or no hope that there's a way out of the battle, a portion of their psyche sits in the waiting room of giving up.

They are as trapped by their system as if they were in a glass box. It's difficult for them to see that a whole system is calling the shots or to know that a system can change. Since the system arises from their implicit memory, they have trouble realizing that this view of the world was *acquired*.

You can't rid yourself of the system entirely, but you can put yourself in situations where it rarely gets activated—and where a safety net catches you before you fall back into the box.

There's a way out of your system. You can find your real life, your true self, and genuine joy—without sacrificing your being. Please read on.

CHAPTER TEN

Mom, Dad, and Anger

Jack was swept along by events: into and out of war, into marriage when a beautiful girl batted her eyes, and into parenthood. One day he woke up and felt like he was in jail. Somehow the entire course of his life had gotten mapped out while he was looking the other way.

Control was important to him. He had controlled himself and made himself do his duty in a terrifying and confusing war. Now he would control himself and make himself work to support his family, not go to college for the education that would let him do the work he wanted, not take the road he had planned to stride.

He was angry. His wonderful wife would try to please him, but he couldn't let himself be pleased. He had too much friction going on inside. He just wanted to do his job, come home, and be left in peace. He couldn't tolerate anybody wanting anything more from him.

Before the war he might have been capable of looking at his wife and seeing her fear when he menaced her. But he'd had to block out a lot to survive the war, and he didn't let perceptions in anymore. He made no effort to read her face. He couldn't stand the little niceties she insisted on. It just made him feel more trapped, so he snarled at her. Then she'd back off, which is what he needed.

He couldn't see what he was doing to her, and she didn't know she didn't have to take it.

Into this tense scene toddled a baby.

Talk about need. Babies need. Jack *really* didn't have the energy for that.

The course of his relationship with his daughter Tamara got set early. She symbolized everything wrong with his life. She needed. She pulled his wife's services from him. She made noise. She cost money. Therefore, she became his target.

Tamara, in her baby vulnerability, felt his hostile energy. He scared her, and she didn't want to get too close. It embarrassed him when she shied away from him, especially in front of others, so he'd punish her.

As she grew up, Jack and Tamara were locked into this pattern. Time only increased his anger, and she was the easiest target in view. If he had a bad day at work, he vented it on her. If traffic was especially snarled, she got yelled at when he came home. Just about anything that caused him anxiety or discomfort got discharged onto her little shoulders.

He couldn't bear it anytime she required extra attention. Normal kid behavior would set him off into a volcano of abuse. Most of the time the abuse was in the form of yelling, loud and long. Sometimes he hit her. Sometimes he would humiliate her.

One day she spilt her milk. He made her get down on the floor and drink milk from a bowl like a dog.

Another time, coming in excited from a softball game, she got mud on the floor. He grabbed her, held her upside down so her eyes were inches from the floor, and paced back and forth, her head dangling, while he yelled at her to look at her footprints.

Any child would be marked by incidents like these. What do you think happens to a vulnerable child treated this way?

Misery addicts, like most addicts, are very perceptive people. They absorb energies from others. They are raw and exposed in a way that normal people aren't. (Hence the need for an addictive behavior or substance. It provides a buffer against the world.)

When treated harshly, sensitive children get afraid to move or act or choose. They stop being kidlike. They erect a radar dish. They make avoiding mistakes a lifestyle. They lose their ability to risk. They get scared to leave the square they are on for an un-known square with hidden dangers. They get afraid to relax. They don't let down their guard. They learn not to hope, not to get excited, not to want anything too much. Sometimes they'll tuck their true selves into a little cave and erect a false self to handle living.

Where was Jack's wife while he was being so mean to Tamara? Marta was right there. She was sitting at the table when he made their child get down on all fours and lap milk from a bowl. She was standing by the door when he hoisted their daughter upside down and dangled her as he paced. She, of course, was the one to sop up the spilled milk and mop the floor.

When he came home in a rage, she watched as he scoured the house to find their daughter, listened as he vented onto Tamara, and saw her daughter's despairing eyes at the dinner table. In the early years, her child had sought Marta's eyes with hope for rescue. None came. Her daughter didn't look toward her anymore.

Marta was passive. She was scared of her husband and believed it was up to her to make the marriage work no matter how much Jack acted against any amiable connection. Jack may have been trying to drive her—and the responsibilities that came with her— away, but their religion did not sanction divorce, so separating didn't seem a real option to either of them.

Marta could not let herself realize that she was sacrificing her daughter. She especially couldn't let herself see, when Jack was going after their daughter, that she, Marta, was somewhat safer. After venting his anger on Tamara, Jack would sink into his chair, have his beer, and read his paper, like a lion easing into a nap.

Tamara had a typical childhood for a misery addict. One parent, usually the father, is critical and angry. The other parent is passive or absent, either unwilling or unable to stop the excesses of the angry spouse.

The abuser can, of course, be the wife and the passive spouse the father. And I've noticed that usually the passive spouse dies first.

Many couples who fit this profile are religious. They can belong to any religion, but in my experience they are more likely to be- long to one in which women are the servers and not normally a part of the church leadership.

Most misery addicts aren't comfortable with their own anger.

Kali Rose had a sweet and winning way, so she attracted friends and people who were generous to her. Often, though, she didn't see or appreciate their generosity. Instead, her attention was on her own internal struggle with self-disapproval and on the current woman from whom she was craving attention and approval.

Most of the time, the woman in her sights had a leadership role in some group Kali Rose was a part of. One such woman was her boss. Another coworker shared the same level of duties as Kali Rose, and she perceived the coworker as the boss's pet and herself as the drudge in their boss's eyes. This replicated her childhood, where her sister was favored by their parents and she was the rejected child.

Kali Rose was fixated on her boss's attention toward the coworker. Anytime Kali Rose believed the other woman was being favored, she would be triggered into the depths of despair, blame herself for her unworthiness, and then binge on junk food. Her primary topic of conversation with friends was the perpetual tempest of her emotions regarding this woman.

One of the first things Kali Rose did when she became part of any group was to assess other members in terms of their closeness to the lead woman. She sorted group members according to these categories: strong women, weak women, competitors, and nonplayers. In addition, she always identified one other group member as her competitor for the lead woman's favor. She was jealous and angry when the leader gave attention to someone else, especially the person she had labeled as her competitor.

In any group, Kali Rose would create an alliance with one other woman, be afraid of her peers who were strong, scapegoat the person she perceived as weakest, and ignore the others. Nonplayers were ignored so thoroughly that even if they asked her a direct question, she might not answer it, as if she neither saw nor heard them. Toward the scapegoated person she would be consistently cutting and dismissive.

The roles she assigned to people shifted if the group shifted. For example, in a church group she attended regularly, she had an alliance with Bettina, a strong woman who was her occasional competitor for the attention of the assistant minister, the leader of the group. In the same group, Kali Rose labeled Evie as weak. However, at a recent church retreat, Kali Rose knew no one except Evie. During the retreat, she poured her considerable charm on Evie in order to form an alliance—one that evaporated by the next Sunday.

People cared enough about her to give her feedback from time to time. When they did, Kali Rose would rapidly descend to a pit of shame, even to the point of being unable to talk. People would then stop giving her feedback and distance themselves from her.

Kali Rose was completely imprisoned by her system. What she wanted most of all was to be with the chosen woman as much as possible. Toward that end, she would do things for her: take on chores, give her back rubs, do odd jobs—anything that gave her extra time with the woman.

Fortunately, most of the time she chose women who were too ethical to take advantage of her. Occasionally, she'd target a woman who would use her. She'd then feel connected to the woman as a result of her services. It wasn't true intimacy, but it felt like a bond. Then when the woman turned her attention to her own life, family, or husband, Kali Rose felt abandoned. And for that she would be furious.

From each phase of this cycle—adoration, despair, sacrifice, abandonment, rage—she got something. Each stage reenacted some aspect of her relationship with her mother.

Misery addicts are often furious. They were not taught healthy ways of handling anger, and they were usually not permitted to show it. To be obviously angry as children would have been too dangerous anyway. In many cases, they would have been seriously punished for it.

They are usually anger-phobic. They abhor looking like the abusive parent, and their fear is that if they open the door to anger, it'll erupt like a volcano, destroy others, and never stop.

Their defenses against anger are solid. This is one aspect of misery addiction that usually requires deep, consistent, focused therapy and group work. The company of warm, safe, intentional people can also help to soften both the anger and the misery addict's defenses against it.

CHAPTER ELEVEN

Protecting Mom (or Dad)

Kali Rose needed protection from her angry dad. She needed her mom, the only other adult in the vicinity, to step in. Her mom did not.

Not only did she not protect Kali Rose, she kept herself at a distance from her. She didn't cuddle Kali Rose or hold her. She was busy concentrating on her angry, high-maintenance husband— and, perhaps, she couldn't let herself stay connected to a child she was not protecting.

Whatever the reason, Kali Rose was on her own.

Kali Rose could not let herself be angry at her mother. After all, her father was the abusive one, not her mom. But she had anger nonetheless. She had a cauldron of anger. So she directed that anger, not at her mom, but at herself. She protected her mother from her own anger.

We've already seen that once a behavior or issue is locked into a misery addict's system, it is solid. Once Kali Rose took on the role of protecting her mother, that role became impervious to logic, reason, or fairness. Protecting her mother then spread into wider territory, like kudzu or buckthorn. Kali Rose didn't just protect her mother from her rage; she tried to minister to her. She tried to give to her.

In adulthood, Kali Rose expanded this role. She kept expending effort to provide for her mother. During her childhood, Kali Rose's protective efforts made it seem like they were connected to each other. In adulthood this was Kali Rose's main currency of connection, but her mom didn't need Kali Rose's protection anymore. Her father and mother had grown used to each other. Her father was no longer mean to her mother, just to Kali Rose.

Kali Rose still could never get into her parents' circle. When she would make efforts toward her mother, her mother didn't see that this was an offering, an invitation. Her mother was still focused on her husband, and Kali Rose was still outside.

Still Kali Rose protected her. Despite the subtle slights and thoughtless, critical remarks her mom made about her, Kali Rose protected her. At holidays and Sunday dinners, when her mother put the bulk of her attention on her husband and her other children, Kali Rose was still focused on her mother, still, in her heart, protecting her.

And when she entered therapy and began to delve into her psyche, Kali Rose protected her.

While replaying over and over her cycle of longing for a particular woman's attention, getting slighted, and responding with rage, Kali Rose protected her mother.

She could let therapy go only so deep. When it started to touch her anger at her mother, therapy had to go. She'd cancel sessions; she'd be late; she'd sabotage herself in some major way that interrupted the therapeutic process.

Protecting her mother was bone deep. She could let nothing touch it.

Another example of a child protecting her mother is seen in the relationship between Tilda and Helena. Tilda was afraid of life. Fear of being alone and unable to support herself and her children kept her living with her angry husband. Fear of doing the wrong thing or making a mistake kept her from taking risks. She passed on this fear to her daughter Helena through the way she treated her.

For example, when Helena was fourteen, a little mole grew on her knee. When her mother saw it, she said in a horrified tone, "Oh! You have a mole," and recoiled from it as if it were a ten-foot python. "You'll never get a husband with a mole like that. We'll have to get it removed."

Tilda did things like this often enough that Helena got the message that her body was revolting and that no one would ever want her.

Yet, as an adult, Helena protected her mother.

Helena could not let herself be angry with her mother for turning her against her own body. Instead she protected her mother and directed her anger against herself through self-critical comments. These sounded very much like the criticisms her mother would say to her.

In Merril's household, her mother was the angry abuser. Dad was passive and did not intervene. Merril couldn't be angry with her dad, so Merril protected her dad by underplaying his role and denying his passivity.

Faced with two models for living—an angry, controlling one and a passive one—she chose to walk the passive route. As an adult, Merril became passive in her response to others and married an emotionally abusive, controlling man.

In other relationships, she was also passive, letting friends and bosses have too much control—which, of course, she resented. She wanted to leave and, at the same time, she felt stuck.

Merril hated anger. She hated what anger had done to her. As a result, she would not let herself feel angry about how her mother had treated her. However, she did allow herself to feel passionately upset at how her mother treated her father. Here is where she allowed some true feeling—on her father's behalf.

Merril discharged some of her anger at her mother through barbed teasing toward her peers. She also found a way to have some power through resistance: she very quietly resisted control and pressure—and help, support, intimacy, therapy, recovery, and liberation. Resistance, even to good things, became part of her system.

Her resistance was greatest when it came to looking at her father's lack of protection from her mother's wrath. She could be somewhat angry *for* her father. But she could not be angry *at* her father. Long after he died, she was still protecting him.

To protect a parent who, even passively, participated in an abusive system creates an internal dilemma. The natural response is to be mad at everyone involved—both the abuser and the people who could have stopped him but didn't.

What does all this have to do with misery addiction?

Protecting either the abuser or the passive adults in a system is itself an act of self-sabotage. Keeping yourself from admitting the truth blocks your process. It interferes with recovery and keeps you stranded.

CHAPTER TWELVE

Body Hate

If there had been an Oscar for "Most Changed by Treatment," Kali Rose would have won it. She arrived at the retreat house at the beginning of the misery addiction treatment program looking like a war refugee.

And she was—a refugee from her war against herself. She had slept just a few hours a night for weeks. She'd eaten nothing but sugary stuff for the previous three days. Exercise? Forget it. And in the span of two hours prior to arriving, she had smoked a pack of cigarettes.

Remember how her father converted his own stress and anxiety into anger against Kali Rose? In a similar way, Kali Rose converted all of her uncomfortable feelings into anger against her own body.

She was over her stress limit when treatment started—changing jobs, worried about a sick friend. Her feelings of being overwhelmed were converted to self-abuse.

Plus she was entering treatment. And nearly everyone binges on their own brand of drug before walking through those life-changing doors.

Now, after two months in the embrace of a healthy community, Kali Rose looked like a different woman. Not permitted to abuse herself, having her human needs met abundantly, she was alert, present, amusing, delightful, and powerful.

After treatment, she moved in with her mother.

"Kali Rose, I thought you were going to the gym. Aren't you late?"

"Kali Rose, when are you going to make something of yourself?"

"Kali Rose, don't sit so close."

"Don't take so long in the bathroom."

"Don't be so messy."

"When are you going to the gym? You said you would leave an hour ago?"

"When are you getting your hair cut?"

"Don't you think it's time to start covering that gray?"

"Now that you are doing so well, why don't you go on a diet? Look, for dinner I made a salad and a cold vegetable plate to help you. You know, when you get older, your metabolism decreases. You have to eat less."

Words like this, spoken at routine intervals, are like slow torture. They send the same message: you are not acceptable.

Would you start feeling irritated if you heard this stuff day in and out? So would anyone. That's the natural reaction.

Kali Rose's mother was picking on her. It would be natural to respond with anger.

But Kali Rose couldn't let herself be angry with her mother, so her self-hatred returned with a vengeance. Within two weeks she was back to staying up too late, bingeing on sugar, skipping medication, and punishing herself.

Kali Rose's mom discharged her own anxiety by targeting Kali Rose; then Kali Rose targeted herself.

Kali Rose would lay down her life for her mother. In a way, she had. By not allowing herself to voice her anger and by abusing her body, Kali Rose was endangering her life.

Another example of a child being turned against his own body is found in Javier's life. Perhaps Graciela resented being a sharecropper's wife. Maybe an exhibitionist unwrapped himself in front of her when she was young. Whatever her reason, she made her son feel dirty.

Javier couldn't escape Graciela's incessant comments to his sister about what all men want, how they just had one thing on their minds, and how she should not let men touch her.

He wouldn't remember her harsh scrubbing when he was diapered, but his implicit memory held the message intact—that women hurt, that the body is a source of pain. He did remember her veiled and embarrassing comments about what he was doing so long in the bathroom and how he had to keep his hands on top of his covers at all times. He remembered the day she refused to wash his sheets and made him do it. He remembered how she wouldn't touch him and recoiled when he hugged her, whether he was seven or twenty-seven.

Javier became an adult with two problems: he hated his body, and he both hated and wanted ministering from women. He expressed his body hatred by putting himself on endless, strict diets. He looked like a prisoner of war. In a way, he was.

His issues with women were complex, so his cycle with women was complex. He had a way of drawing a woman to him, inviting her to mother him, and then stripping her of her self-esteem with brilliant, undetectable insults. He picked needy women with low self-esteem who would never leave him, and then he left them.

Not all misery addicts hate and target their bodies, but those who do have one thing in common—their mothers rejected them physically and criticized their appearance, movement, or sexuality. In addition, their mothers were not usually physically affectionate. They didn't cuddle, hug, or hold their children.

Every child is in serious need of a stamp of approval from Mom. She's the maker after all. If your manufacturer finds you faulty, it's hard to overcome the stigma. It makes you feel like she regrets putting you together.

Any reasons she might have—such as not wanting to be pregnant or being upset at losing her career—don't help. By the time you learn this information, you've already lived with rejection for at least a couple of decades.

Maternal rejection seeps into our cells. We are filled with a sense of wrongness that isn't easily overcome.

One lever that will pry it loose is expressing our anger fluently and flowingly. We don't have to express it to the person with whom we are angry. We just have to say it to someone who cares about us and who will listen heartfully. We may have to pound a pillow or throw ice at a wall outside, but pillows don't get hurt and ice melts.

It's important for everyone to express anger and to be willing and able to do so. But most of the misery addicts I've worked with have stuck anger, anger that is suppressed and difficult to access. Yet even deeply buried anger finds some way to pollute the ground. It's either misdirected to an inappropriate target, such as our own body, or expressed indirectly through passive aggression, passive resistance, hurtful teasing, or sabotage.

People who mishandle anger in the opposite direction, through rage or violence, usually aren't misery addicts, and they're more likely to harm others than themselves. The emotion they are suppressing is commonly grief or fear. (For these folks I recommend the books *The Anger Habit* by Carl Semmelroth and Donald Smith and *Beyond Anger—A Guide for Men: How to Free Yourself from the Grip of Anger and Get More Out of Your Life* by Thomas Harbin.)

In either case, a true feeling is being redirected into a different expression that feels more acceptable. Unfortunately, however, stand-ins never do the trick. If grief is the true feeling, rage won't diminish it. If anger is the true feeling, no amount of misdirected, indirect anger will abate it.

Only a clear, direct, wholehearted expression of the anger will do the job.

CHAPTER THIRTEEN

Double Trouble

A misery addict has a hard enough life. She doesn't deserve the pain of other addictions or conditions.

If only life were fair.

Most misery addicts deal with at least one other big-time difficulty. Kali Rose has chemically caused depression and attention deficit disorder (ADD). Helena has depression. Merril is dysthymic and has dissociative disorder. Sanderson is an alcoholic.

Did the other disorder contribute to these people's misery addiction? Perhaps.

In the case of ADD, it's a real possibility. Parents of children with undiagnosed attention deficit disorder often get overwhelmed and irritated when their children keep forgetting things, including the rules. Their frustration can feel like rejection. They can become too angry.

When alcoholics become sober, they are often surprised to discover that they have another disorder, one that was buried underneath the alcoholism. In fact, their slide into alcoholism may have been an unconscious attempt to medicate that disorder.

With misery addiction, which came first? In the case of a misery addict with depression, did the depression cause the misery addiction, or did the negative consequences from the misery addiction cause the depression? It's difficult to say.

We know that trauma can cause physically based depression.

Childhood trauma messes up the brain's soothing systems, and the body needs some outside source to make up for the deficit. Alcohol, drugs, food, and excessive exercise can be the tools for this.

In terms of treatment, it doesn't matter which came first. Each of the issues requires attention. Regardless of which disorder led to which, a misery addict will use the sister disorder in the service of the misery addiction.

Thus recovery from misery addiction may not take hold if the other disorder goes untreated. Certainly a drinking alcoholic isn't going to have a mind clear enough for the penetrating work of misery addiction recovery. Yet if the misery addiction isn't attended to in a timely fashion, the improvements wrought by sobriety could trigger a relapse back to drinking.

A person with untreated depression might not have the energy to take all the steps recovery requires. Untreated ADD may interrupt a person's ability to sustain his focus on the steps required for recovery.

So treatment for sister disorders must proceed in concert with the recovery process.

GIVE THEM A PILL

Why didn't I think of that?

Actually there are pills for most of these other disorders. But we're talking misery addiction here. If a person is addicted to misery, is she going to take a pill that makes her feel better?

That's the catch.

There are numerous effective treatments for depression these days. If you're depressed, you picked the right century for it. But misery addicts are notorious for wanting to discontinue their depression medication. And they'll pick the worst time to do it.

In the Pacific Northwest, for example, it's seriously dark in the winter. Winter is not the season to throw away your Prozac.

How about when your husband leaves you? Or when you discover your wife's having an affair? Would that be a good time?

When you're changing jobs and shouldn't be rocking your emotional boat, how about then?

Get the picture?

A misery addict's thing is self-sabotage. If a medication will help a condition, a misery addict's tendency is to keep going off that medication, and at the worst possible time.

CHAPTER FOURTEEN

Stopped

STOPPED BY FEELINGS

Brett had yearned to create ceramic art for as long as she could remember. She talked about it often, and when she did, you could see her longing in her face.

Her friends, wanting to help, gathered round her with suggestions. One of them offered her the following list:

1. Get started somehow: look in the newspaper, in the Yellow Pages, or on the Web for classes.
2. Sign up for something, anything: a class, a workshop, an Artist's Way group.
3. While you're inspired by the energy of the class, talk to the instructor and other students about various ways to connect with the art world.
4. Visit the closest art school, talk to some faculty, and look at its catalog and Web site, including its listing of community education or extension classes.
5. If you like what you see, find out how to sign up for a ceramics class.
6. Sign up!
7. If you feel overwhelmed at any point, get support to continue from a friend who backs you up in your vision.

"That looks overwhelming," said Brett.

Saffron nodded. "It is too much to think of at once. Just pick one step, a way to get started. Sometimes the hardest part is getting started."

Tom said, "Do a Web search for art classes."

Brett responded, "That's a good idea. But I don't know how to do a Web search."

"I can teach you," said Tom. "It's easy to learn."

"Okay," said Brett. "But I don't feel that I can begin until I have a space to work in."

Get the picture? Brett always had a reason for not starting toward her dream.

What was really going on here?

Brett was scared. She found a roadblock for every solution because she was scared. She was stopped by a feeling.

Feelings are deeply important. They need to be heard, understood, accepted, and addressed, but they are not a reason to avoid the steps that will take you where you want to go in your life.

If you have a misery addiction, however, fear is no small, occasional feeling; it can be an ongoing, subtle current that influences you constantly. Yet you may not consciously feel it.

Brett wasn't actually conscious of the fear that kept her from acting. She perceived it more as inertia. Yet whenever she took the slightest action toward change, she'd be stopped as if a barrier had dropped across her path. She'd be frozen without actually experiencing the fear behind it. Brett protected herself from fear through inertia.

– Exercise 2: What Feeling Stops You? –

The purpose of this exercise is to find out more about the feelings that can keep you from reaching out to fulfill your desires.

First, consider the following situation; then answer the questions about the feelings that came up for you.

(You don't have to actually define what your deepest desire is or figure out what the path is to get there.)

Imagine . . . before you is the path to the life that, in your deepest heart, you want to enjoy.

Now imagine that all you have to do to get started on this path is to make a phone call—a local call. (Yes, you know the number, and yes, your phone works fine.)

Questions for Journaling or Talking with a Friend

As you imagined the path to joy, what did you feel? What did you want to do?

As you imagined making a call to get started on the path, what did you want to do?

What did you feel?

Would that feeling keep you from making the call?

Does that feeling keep you from doing things you want to do?

Can you remember experiencing that feeling when you were a child?

Can you remember an incident in your childhood that caused that feeling?

Challenge Yourself

Feel the feeling that makes you want to skip this exercise; then do the exercise anyway.

Afterward, list the things you learned about yourself.

If willing, write about the whole process you went through or discuss your process with a friend, therapist, or recovery group.

STOPPED BY A SMALL TASK

Colin loved to bike. He loved to sail over country roads with the wind in his hair, sit at a wayside rest with a cheese and apple sandwich, take an off-road dirt path to a private showing of nature's artwork.

Yet each year, after the snow melted for the last time, he collided with the same impasse. He'd feel defeated by the idea of getting his equipment ready for biking.

If we look at this with logic, we can't get anywhere. All he had to do was pump air into the bike's tires, put the bike rack on his car, and make sure his saddlebags were equipped. The whole show took less than thirty minutes. Once the equipment was ready, he'd have a whole summer of joy. Thirty minutes versus an entire summer—a no-brainer.

Yet year after year, he'd be delayed for weeks, even months, by feeling overwhelmed at the preparation involved. When he would finally break through his inertia, get his equipment ready, and get out on the road, he'd wonder why it took him so long. He was enjoying himself so much. It was so easy. Preparation didn't take any time at all.

One fall, to assist himself, he created a special space for all his bike equipment. He organized it on racks, all in one place, clean and ready to go.

Still, when the next spring rolled around, he was overcome by his usual feelings. One year its grip was so strong he missed an entire summer of biking.

Months of joy aborted by avoidance of a half hour's work.

This is another signal of misery addiction.

What's going on? Here are some possibilities:

- It could be another manifestation of being stopped by a feeling—in this case, the feeling of joy. For Colin, joy is risky, because when it stops, he doesn't have joy anymore. To prevent a slide down and out of joy, Colin may keep himself from getting joyful in the first place.
- Colin can be scared that if he relaxes, something—some person or event or feeling—will swallow him. When Colin is biking, he's relaxed and peaceful. He may be unwilling to get too relaxed. Being relaxed makes him vulnerable, so Colin feels safer staying on guard.
- Dangers posed by the activity can metaphorically reenact a childhood dilemma. For example, Colin felt stranded in his family during childhood. He can unknowingly be scared of any experience that has the potential of stranding him. To have the old family metaphor reenacted yet again seems unbearable. Such a fear, probably unfelt, would be another case of implicit memory at work, anticipating a dread Colin isn't even able to name.
- Colin might feel that others may ridicule or abandon him— for his passion, for how he looks on a bike, if he bikes with a jock friend who can pedal twice as fast.

- Colin might be afraid to trust his body to have the skill or stamina required. Some misery addicts can come to believe as children that their bodies are at fault for the bad things that happened to them. They then tell themselves that if they had a different body, those bad things wouldn't have happened. Also, a physical activity increases our contact with our bodies. If Colin has detached himself from his body in order to keep from feeling painful emotions, he will try to avoid doing something that involves exercise.

- Perhaps as a child, Colin didn't have a secure base from which to explore. As a result, he may be fearful of exploration as an adult. If exploratory behavior was punished by Colin's parents when he was young, then physically exploring (such as through biking) or metaphorically exploring (such as by taking an art class) can unwittingly activate a fear of punishment.

STOPPED BY SIGNIFICANCE

Anjali, raised by a traditional mother, learned the home-keeping arts well. Her culture delineated female roles precisely. To Anjali's mother, being an attorney was not one of Anjali's options.

In America, Anjali was schooled at a small villagelike enclave with compatriot girls. Her exposure to American culture was carefully limited. However, she loved to read and from reading knew about the wider world. She also felt strongly about justice and fairness.

She had many fears, based on a harsh father and a cowering mother. But she also had a teacher who believed in her and who saw the incisive intelligence hiding under meek chestnut eyes.

Over time, Anjali confided her dreams to her teacher, and her teacher began honing her lessons to prepare her for a university. Her teacher also began meeting with Anjali's parents, gradually preparing them to take in broader concepts of their daughter's potential.

When it came time to take the test that could give her entry to that world, Anjali suffered from much fear. She wasn't afraid of stepping outside her culture. That idea excited her. She wasn't afraid of taking control of her own life. She'd been chomping at that bit for a decade. What made her falter was that she was approaching a door that could go exactly where she wanted to go. The test represented so much fulfillment for her that it terrified her to take it.

Many of us know about the fear that accompanies the steps toward our wildest dreams. It's scary to allow ourselves to have enough hope to keep traveling that direction. It's so hard to believe that what we most want could actually work out.

Yet we have those dreams for a reason. We vibrate in that direction on purpose, because that's our signpost toward our life's intention.

If a normal person finds it difficult to step in that direction, you can imagine how tough it is for people addicted to misery. Just thinking about their dreams can increase their anxiety, and anxiety sends them toward their tool addictions. Thus at the most opportune time for taking an action toward their dreams, they are in peril of doing the most sabotaging thing.

This is damaging for misery addicts and frustrating for the people who love them. Over time, when friends see their assistance spurned or their supportive actions undone, they may lose their energy for helping.

It is so common to feel anxious about stepping toward an important dream that this characteristic alone cannot be used to diagnose a person as being addicted to misery. However, if you know that you are addicted to misery, then the time to be especially vigilant about using your recovery support system is when you are moving toward what you desire.

CHAPTER FIFTEEN

The Tie That Unravels

"Simone, you ate too much chicken. I made that extra for myself for lunch tomorrow."

"It was on the dinner table."

"I know, but it wasn't for you. Now I won't have anything to eat tomorrow. Don't you ever think of anyone but yourself? Your father will have to punish you for your greed."

"How was I supposed to know, Mama? If you needed it, why didn't you set it aside instead of serving it on the platter?"

"Now he'll have to punish you for talking back."

Many years later Simone came into my office and looked at me warily.

"I can tell something's wrong," I said, gesturing for her to have a seat. "What is it?"

"You changed our appointment time."

"Yes, I did."

"Why?"

"A crown came off my tooth and that was the only time my dentist could see me."

"You could have gone to a different dentist, one who had a different time available." (Notice that this is a version of what her mother would do—thinking of something Simone wouldn't have naturally thought of, to make her feel in the wrong.)

"Yes, I could have. What does it mean to you that I changed our time?"

She looked away and then moved just her eyes to peek at me from the corners. "I thought you were setting me up," she said in a small voice.

"To what end?"

"I thought you were changing the time to upset me and to see what I would do."

"Hmmm." I paused while I felt into the consciousness of the little girl inside her who was having this reaction. "That must have been scary, thinking I was changing things just to make you feel bad."

"It was . . ." And from there she went deeper into her own process—which was, of course, about her mother.

Many times she would misperceive me as trying to set her up in order to make her hurt. This is natural to the therapeutic process, to project onto the therapist the motives and intentions of the parent.

In case the term isn't familiar, a *projection* is a belief you have about another person's intentions or feelings that comes out of your own history. It's a coloration you add to the relationship. If your father was always angry, then to your eyes a man in authority might always look angry, even if he actually isn't. The problem is that we tend to proceed from a projection into behavior that doesn't fit the situation. For example, if you assume your boss is angry when he isn't, you might be argumentative when it isn't called for, or excessively meek.

When you project your family history onto someone else, you are creating a story about that person that may not be true.

Of course, a wounded person doesn't restrict his projections to the therapist, who knows (or at least, ought to know) how to handle them. Usually he projects onto everyone—his spouse or partner, his boss, the government, women, men, friends, his children, coworkers, people in authority, the guy in the next car.

This is of great importance for misery addicts because the single most important facet of recovery, other than abstinence from addictive behaviors and substances, is getting and using support from others. They need others, but they tend to act according to their own projections, which can mystify their friends and drive them away.

Ingrid, with her lightning intelligence, longs to be connected, and the method she uses is to read what others need and provide it. This, as we've seen before, has created a cadre of friends organized around what she gives. In the midst of these sucklings, she is lonely. When someone tries to give to her, she resists so forcefully that generous people back off.

Of course, this same pattern shows up in her therapeutic relationship. She resists taking in my regard for her. I offer her opportunities for connection, and she redirects them. She is skilled, smooth, and so delightful that I could miss realizing that I just got diverted if I weren't paying attention. I'm struck at how imprisoned she is within this pattern.

Why would a person suffering from loneliness prevent closeness?

It is not at all what she wants. She understands fully what she is doing. And bright as she is, she is powerless inside it.

How does a person get so trapped by a pattern? Why isn't it possible to just go, "Oh, I get it. If I do this, it messes me up. I'll stop doing it"?

If only it were that easy. Therapy and recovery would take one week, and we could all go boating.

After caring so deeply about Ingrid, I finally realized I cared too much. Ingrid is fearful of people who are invested in her. It doesn't matter that my investment is positive and that I'm on her side. She's been accustomed to people being invested in her for their benefit, not hers. Her sister and her mother were both invested in having Ingrid meet their needs and sacrifice her own.

Though Ingrid has a home, job, friends, and activities in another state, her mother still wonders when Ingrid will move back to Kansas City to be with her. Her mother makes no recognition of the life Ingrid has built away from her.

No wonder Ingrid sees family as a trap. As much as she longs for connection, she doesn't want to give anyone the power of taking so much from her again. Paradoxically, Ingrid needs me to care less.

The work of thousands of people has brought forth a body of knowledge to help us understand the fixed nature of our relationships. This work is called attachment theory, and it arose from the observations and writings of John Bowlby, who got kicked out by the Freudians for his audacious ideas.[1]

Since Bowlby's original splash in the 1950s, research has fanned out in so many directions that it is now possible to make reasonable predictions about the probable (but *not* inevitable) issues of the grandchildren of a child who is not yet born.

The research that catapulted attachment theory forward began with Mary Ainsworth, who constructed an ingenious method for observing infant attachment behavior. Called the Strange Situation,[2] it works like this: a parent and a twelve-month-old infant are placed alone in a room with toys. An adult stranger enters, is introduced, and joins the child in play. The parent leaves for a few minutes, then returns, and soon thereafter the stranger leaves quietly. After a bit, the parent again leaves the room; the stranger enters again and plays with the child for a few minutes more; then the parent returns and the stranger leaves. Thus there are two separations and two reunions.

Observations from these studies were correlated with data collected in home visits and intensive interviews with the parents. From thousands of such studies, the components of secure and insecure attachment have been fine-tuned.[3]

Mothers of secure infants respond promptly to a crying child, holding the baby tenderly and carefully and providing tactful, cooperative guidance (or distraction when maternal and infant desires conflict).[4] A secure child uses his mother as a secure base for exploring the room, checking on her from time to time, but exploring the toys.

At the first separation, a baby may cry and be less interested in play. Some infants are comforted by the presence of the stranger. When Mom returns, she is clearly preferred, and most secure children will go to her, seek contact, and be comforted by the contact. When sufficiently soothed, a secure infant is then able to return to play. Even when not distressed, however, a secure child responds to Mom's return, greeting her with a smile or some interaction.[5]

Insecure attachments are formed when an infant is forced to habitually employ defensive behaviors to protect herself from a parent who has an insufficient grasp of the child's emotional state.[6]

A secure child achieves a comfortable balance between contact (intimacy) and exploration (autonomy). An insecure child ends up sacrificing one for the other. With a dismissive parent, a child sacrifices intimacy and becomes avoidant. With a needy, inept, or preoccupied parent, a child sacrifices autonomy.

THE NATURE OF ATTACHMENT

Right after we are born, we want to connect with somebody. We'll look for it from anyone who takes care of us, but we narrow our focus quickly to the person who is most responsive to us when we cry and who interacts most with us—usually Mom. The quality of that interaction establishes two things for us: a secure base and a safe haven.[7]

We need a secure base from which to launch our exploration of the world, and we need a safe haven to run back to when the world gets scary. For newborns, everything rests on one thing: is our mom sensitive to our signals?[8]

Our security hinges on this. If she's paying attention, reads us accurately, and responds effectively, we become secure. If she's insensitive and responds ineffectively, we become insecure.

From such small acorns do mighty oaks grow. It might seem unfair that an entire life gets directed on the basis of these first delicate interactions. (And there are certainly other factors that can improve a baby's lot—for example, an involved support community for the mother, a happy marriage, an attentive dad, or contact with some other loving, effective caregiver.)

Still, fair or not, the quality of a parent's care and responsiveness during the first couple of months of a baby's life are decisive. From the thousands of studies on attachment behavior, we have a way to understand the different routes a baby takes when some of this goes wrong.

AVOIDANT ATTACHMENT

Ingrid demonstrates one of the options—avoidant attachment. Even without an understanding of the events of her childhood, we can see this from her behavior in therapy. Stored in her implicit memory, she has a model of relationships from which she operates in any association.

Yesterday Ingrid came to her therapy group referring to a day of weeping. It was unusual for her to let herself cry, and even more so to let us in on it, so her disclosure was welcomed. Encouraged to talk, she allowed her face to show her sadness, and throughout her talking, she would make warding-off gestures with her hands, as if deflecting blows. She would cut herself short and stop herself when her feelings swelled, interrupting herself with self-blaming remarks.

At one point, I asked her if she expected us to be critical of her sadness. The group united in support of her, and her warding-off gestures decreased. Yet she would not let herself express her full sadness or receive comfort from us.

This is common among adults who, feeling insecurely attached as babies, developed an avoidant mode of attaching to others in order to reduce the pain of an inattentive caregiver. Giovanni Liotti put it this way:

> Whenever patients seem paradoxically to avoid emotional proximity to the therapist when they are more distressed, the therapist may hypothesize that they are reenacting an old pattern of avoidant attachment. Therefore, the therapist may also assume that these patients, whenever they feel distressed, are prone to tacitly construe themselves as unworthy of attention and to expect to be rejected by the therapist if they ask for his or her attention.[9]

The therapy process thus uncannily replicates the course of a baby's first experiences of distress.

Imagine being a baby. Something's wrong—a wet diaper or an empty stomach. You're distressed and you cry. The crying is a signal to your caregiver. It is also a signal to you. The communication you send outward is also reverberating inside of you. You hear your own distress, and as a result, your distress intensifies.

The response to your cry from your caregiver determines what you do next.

Consider this reaction from Mom:

"Oh my precious darling. Something is wrong. That's your hungry cry. You need to eat." And with that, Mom picks you up and starts feeding you.

Her words are indicative of her thought process, that she is paying attention and thinking about what need your cry is signaling and how to meet that need. Her response contains your distress.

A mom who is on the ball helps her baby learn to associate distress with the possibility of its alleviation and thus strengthens the baby's capacity to tolerate uncomfortable feelings. His confidence that he will be cared for is increased.

In contrast, ask yourself how this would feel:

"Oh, I get so upset when you cry. I'm so busy. I don't have time for this. There's nothing really wrong with you. I'll just stick this bottle in your mouth so I can get back to my work."

Your distress wouldn't be contained, would it? You'd get physical nourishment, but not emotional soothing.

Notice how the second mom's reaction is different right off the bat. Her response is about herself. The baby's cry causes an increase in her own anxiety, not in her urge to nurture. She isn't able to turn her attention to her baby's experience. Instead she moves into a defense *against* the baby—in this case, avoiding the baby with work.

Dr. Peter Fonagy explains this situation eloquently: "If the child learns that he cannot rely on the mother to respond to the signals of his negative affective states and to reduce them, he . . . must find alternative ways to diminish them. . . . The child internalizes perception of the mother's reaction to his own affective signals."[10]

Thus the baby internalizes—that is, takes on—Mom's defenses. This mom's reaction is to avoid distress, so her baby will also learn to avoid distress.

Many, many studies show that defenses are passed on from parent to child. If Dad's defense (say, against anxiety or grief) is anger, it's likely that his child's defense will be anger. If Mom's defense (say, against her own anger) is fear, it's likely her child will be fearful.

Of course, I'm not talking here about a single interaction but a pattern of interactions. No mom can be 100 percent attentive.

Even good moms are inconsistent. And if a mom has sufficient help, then her overall attentiveness and responsiveness can increase. The point of this information is not to blame mothers, but to help us see how our lives have been determined in part by these early interactions.

Here is the above sequence shown visually:

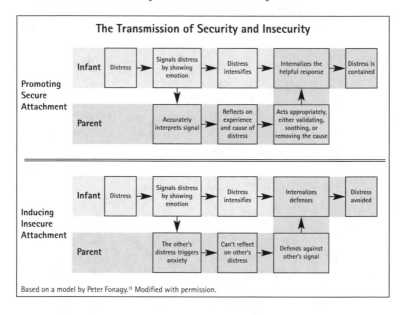

Based on a model by Peter Fonagy.[11] Modified with permission.

Ingrid, in her response to therapy, replicated, and therefore revealed, the usual sequence in her early life. Her expression of distress led to further, intensified distress, which she then avoided, usually through self-blame.

What went on in her household when she was a baby? Mom and Dad both worked long hours, and her older sister Anja saw Ingrid as an intruder. Anja would then capture parental attention by acting out and by making demands. Ingrid got only the leftovers.

Remember, Anja was often left in charge of Ingrid, and she resented it. She blamed Ingrid for being born and for increasing the household demands for money and space, thereby causing their parents to work harder.

Of course Anja was, through her own actions, showing that

she'd also been underparented. Her behavior made it clear that parental attention was scarce, so she saw Ingrid as her competitor. She made sure to win most contests with her younger sister, and Ingrid adapted by choosing not to need—anything.

Sitting in the therapy group, warding off expected criticism with her little hands, interjecting frequent comments of self-blame, Ingrid demonstrated well her childhood experience.

A circle capable of intimacy—Ingrid's therapy and recovery groups—sent her into anxiety. All of her techniques went on red alert. She was busy letting others go first, responding to their needs, giving them supportive feedback. It took time, attentiveness, and consistent acceptance for her to begin to settle in and will take more time as she tentatively accepts gradations in enhanced closeness.

To summarize, one adaptation a baby can make when her attachment to Mom is insecure is to become attached in a limited, avoidant manner. She appears minimally interested in what Mom is doing, as if she hardly realizes she's there, and explores busily. If Mom leaves the room, she shows minimal distress, and when Mom comes back, she ignores or avoids her.[12]

In fact, when Mom returns, the baby may look or turn away and may even reach for a toy as he hears Mom approaching. If Mom picks him up, his body may stiffen, but he still shows no feeling, leaning out and pointing to a toy. When put down, he moves away and renews his attention to the toys. So in lieu of being close to Mom, the baby involves himself with his toys.

What's happening inside that baby? His heart rate jumps when Mom leaves, and his cortisol levels (stress indicators) elevate when Mom returns. The baby looks like he isn't noticing, but his body tells a different story. While showing no outward signs, he is internally distressed.[13]

Further studies have revealed that avoidance of the mother is specifically linked to the mother's rejection of the infant's attempts to attach to her. Mothers of such infants reported their dislike of touching, and they have been observed actively rebuffing their infants in response to their bids for intimacy and withdrawing from their infants when their children seemed sad.[14]

Ingrid wants closeness, but as she passes a certain point toward intimacy, her anxiety rises so high that she can risk no further. Her anxiety increases because her body remembers—her implicit memory remembers—the constellation of events that occurred when, as a baby, she tried to get close. Her primary caregivers left, either emotionally or physically. And then she was left in the care of someone without affection for her, someone who saw her as a rival and who was mean-spirited and punitive.

She has arranged her entire life around preventing the anxiety and risk of counting too much on someone. She tries to surround herself with people who won't leave her because of all she does for them. And if they do leave her, well, she wasn't that attached to them anyway.

In this way, Ingrid actively sabotages intimacy, which causes her to feel unfulfilled but safe.

Misery addicts with avoidant, distant, or rejecting moms are more likely to turn to a form of busyness when distressed. This busyness gives them a sense of pseudo-security. It isn't true security, but it feels like it because, in infancy, it was. Exploring and toys were the substitute for a mom who didn't engage, so in adulthood busyness is soothing.

Ingrid, after a stressful day, would race to the computer and play games for hours, having difficulty tearing herself away.

Misery addicts with this type of background are likely to turn to tool addictions that involve compulsive activity—overworking, compulsive cleaning, excessive game-playing, and compulsive shopping.

When this kind of misery addict stops working, due to a vacation or a situation where busyness is not possible, his anxiety rises. He will find some way to do something in order to alleviate his anxiety and return to that state of pseudo-security.

AMBIVALENT/PREOCCUPIED/RESISTANT

Avril called her therapist for the third time that week. "I wanted to call because I got a letter from my ex, and I didn't know how to handle it."

"Avril, remember the boundary. You can call me once a week—no more. And we just spoke two days ago. We will handle these issues at our therapy session tomorrow."

"I know you said that, but I was real upset by what my ex said in the letter."

"Bring the letter to your session tomorrow."

Avril's session the next day was her last before her therapist left for her annual one-month vacation. Her anxiety had been growing as her therapist's vacation approached.

During the vacation, she still had her therapy group with a substitute therapist. The substitute was familiar to the group, and the group members themselves offered connection to each other. Still, even though it was an environment of support and continuity, Avril missed half of the group sessions and refused to be drawn out by the substitute.

When her therapist returned, Avril was tearful and very upset. She complained repeatedly about the substitute therapist. She was tearful and unhappy, and all of her therapist's best efforts failed to soothe her. Occasionally Avril would take a quick dig at the therapist but would immediately follow that with a rapid speech about how important the therapist was to her. At the end of the session, she tried to prolong their time together, coming up with new issues as she walked toward the door. Just before Avril left, she told the therapist how great and helpful she was.

Avril's therapy had a tidal pattern. Her commitment waxed and waned. When some sort of separation from her therapist approached, Avril would become very focused on her therapist and draw near to her. But when Avril could have scheduled a long stretch of sessions in a row without a break, she would cancel sessions, saying she was too busy for therapy.

Her life reflected a similar pattern. She was very focused on people when they weren't there and effusive when they first returned. But then she would disappear. Just as they were getting quite close, she'd withdraw and have some excuse for avoiding get-togethers. And when someone distressed or upset her, she was not easily soothed.

In the Strange studies (when infants were separated from their moms and a stranger entered the room), it wasn't the child's behavior as Mom left that was most telling, but the child's reactions on Mom's return. These differed strikingly, making it possible to identify the varieties of insecure attachment.

As we've seen, avoidant infants ignored Mom's leaving and returning. In contrast, a second category, preoccupied infants, focused on Mom at all times, seeking contact and proximity even before her departure. They were wary of both the strange room and the unfamiliar person.

While their mothers were gone, these infants got quite distressed, weren't soothed by the stranger, and wanted immediate contact when Mom returned. Yet they weren't calmed by the contact. The hallmark of this classification was seeking contact but resisting angrily once it was achieved, showing ambivalence.[15]

What was going on with the mothers of these ambivalent, preoccupied infants? *They were preoccupied themselves.* They were inept at holding their babies, unpredictable, and rarely tender and careful. They often couldn't match their pacing to their babies'.[16] They discouraged autonomy and were insensitive to infant signals and communications.[17] Mothers were both over- and under-responsive, sometimes neglecting their children, other times overwhelming them.[18]

As a result, the baby thinks, *I need this person, but she's rough with me. I try to get her attention, and she doesn't get what I'm saying. I'm angry at having to depend on her. Yet I get so little; I better hang close. If I wander too far, I might miss my chance at getting something. But if I get too close, she might engulf me. I can't ever tell which way it'll be. Boy, this makes me mad.*

The baby is in an approach/avoidance situation. She approaches, but she usually doesn't get what she needs, and she gets angry. By the age of one, this is the baby's pattern.

Such a background often leads to the anxious world of misery addiction.

What are these parents preoccupied with? In most cases, they are preoccupied with their own parents and the events of their own childhoods.

Avril, in her interactions with both her loved ones and her therapist, demonstrated many behaviors connected to ambivalent attachment—preoccupation, difficulty being soothed, and anger.

A misery addict with this type of attachment disorder may have difficulty letting something work. She may put herself in a treatment program and then resist it, go to therapy and then not do any assignments, see the doctor and then toss out the prescription. She wants relief but doesn't want to—can't bear to—lose her autonomy, such as it is.

Ambivalence can show up in indecision: I want to; I don't. I'll go; I'll stay. All the back and forth activity can use up a lot of time and waste options.

Some misery addicts get very focused on one thing—a person, a fantasy, a past mistake—and are unable to turn their attention to much else, missing equally good opportunities that drift by. They may be limited in their ability to play or explore and may be fearful of risk.

DISORGANIZED AND DISORIENTED

Kali Rose called her therapist before her session. "I have a list of things I want to talk about today. I especially want to talk about what's happening at work."

Thus primed, the therapist waited expectantly as Kali Rose sat down. And then they waited together. Kali Rose said nothing and wouldn't look at her therapist.

"I got your message. I know you wanted to talk about work. What's happening there?"

She was silent, still looking down.

"Did something happen after you left the message? Did something upset you?"

More silence.

Silences like this weren't unusual for Kali Rose. Her expression would vary—sometimes brooding, other times vexed. She would start sentences and then not finish them.

Compare Kali Rose's actions with the behaviors of infants revealing the third classification of adaptations made by insecure children:[19]

- contradictory behaviors
- incomplete and interrupted expressions
- asymmetrical and mistimed movements
- freezing, stilling, and slowed movements and expressions
- apprehension

These infants could neither respond to nor approach their parents, yet they couldn't fully shift their attention away either. Thus they used both the previous two strategies—avoidance and resistance—in a disorganized fashion. Sometimes the opposing impulses clashed, and they froze.

While Kali Rose was being silent with her therapist, on the inside she was deafened by a cacophony. She froze because she was so bombarded by contradictory impulses that she couldn't move.

Like the infants who were disoriented by their mothers' return, Kali Rose experienced distress upon any reunion with her therapist. She was replicating the behavior of a disorganized, disoriented infant.

How do children get this way? Mary Main describes the critical factor that worsens a child's lot considerably: Neither "consistent, unalarming levels of rejection . . . nor unpredictable responsiveness is likely in itself to lead to infant disorganized attachment status, unless the caregiver is also frightening."[20]

A child's attachment strategy deteriorates when her parent becomes frightening or alarming. Understandably, a child would freeze when frightened by her own parent. After all, a frightened child naturally turns toward Mom. But if Mom is frightening, she's stuck.

That a child is caused distress by an abusive parent is not surprising. However, it turns out that a *frightened* parent is *also* alarming and leaves the child without a strategy for living.[21]

A critical parent and a frightened parent are *both* frightening. The critical parent alarms the child, and the frightened parent offers no strategy. The child is, psychically, on his own.

This explains the misery addict who freezes, who can't act in time to take advantage of a good thing.

Many misery addicts come from homes with one angry, abusive, or critical parent and one passive, victimized, or fearful parent. No wonder so many misery addicts petrify when action is required.

Now, what about intimacy with yourself? Self-intimacy includes being connected to your own feelings, letting yourself know your deepest desires, honoring your dreams, spending time with yourself, and taking in the beauties of nature. If intimacy with others is an issue, do you imagine that intimacy with self is also going to be an issue?

Of course. When we carry fear or anger, we can be alarming to ourselves. The same approach/avoidance confusion experienced with others can also occur within our own bodies. We can get frozen or put into a trancelike state by anything that increases our self-awareness—which is, of course, exactly what therapy is designed to do. Thus a person may enter therapy with great hopes, only to freeze inside the session or start resisting like mad.

For such a person, attachment to something other than a human being starts to make a lot of sense. If you freeze up when you approach intimacy with humans, you can find some (false) relief and security at the bar, restaurant, casino, workplace, gym, mall, or computer. Mix or match, it doesn't matter. These connections won't reject you, turn a cold shoulder, engulf you, or be seriously inconsistent.

The harm from these pseudo-intimate connections, both in their direct cost and in the indirect bleeding of energy and attention, may be so obvious to friends on the outside that they can't help but urge moderation or abstinence. Therapists will chant the same mantra and urge the use of support from live human beings. But these voices don't soak in very far because they are bucking the misery addict's surrogate attachment: her brilliant solution to the frozen wasteland between autonomy and intimacy.

RISK

Much of the self-sabotage exhibited by a misery addict can be seen as a fear of risking that has spread far beyond the original territory of protection.

A new human begins his first steps of interaction with the world through exploration. First a baby explores his toys, then an infant explores his room and the interesting things in it, a toddler explores his yard and other children, a child explores his neighborhood and the interests of his mind, a teenager explores his town and relationships, and an adult explores the world and whatever it holds that captivates him.

A healthy human being's life is marked by these ever-widening circles of exploration. The first steps in this lifelong process are taken by the infant, who tries to maintain a delicate balance between exploration and proximity to her parent or caregiver, especially when exploration proves threatening. Warmth and security from the caregiver buoy the infant to return to exploration.

A child's security is based on her perception of the availability and competence of her caregiver when she needs comfort or protection. The child then organizes her responses based on her perceptions. As Nancy Weinfield explains, "Infants with secure attachment relationships are confident in the sensitive and responsive availability of their caregivers, and consequently these infants are confident in their own interactions with the world."[22]

When a child feels insecure, that insecurity interferes with his exploration. An avoidant child will be fearful of exploring intimacy as an adult. A resistant, preoccupied child will be hesitant to risk other kinds of exploration as an adult. By adulthood, the arena seen as risky can cover sizeable territory.

Frequently, the self-sabotage of a misery addict takes the form of what is *not* done. The form is not sent in on time; the appointment is not made; the resume is not updated; the words are not said; the feelings are not felt; the therapist, sponsor, or support group is not reached out to.

The person's fear of risking has become generalized to include most steps or actions that expand outward. The paralysis of that long-ago infant is still operating in the adult's life.

This is one reason why a recovery process must accompany therapy for anyone with more than a mild case of misery addiction. A good therapist is completely available to provide a secure base and a safe haven during appointments. The rest of the time, however, misery addicts need an accepting and available community to help them keep a sense of security alive. Using the structure of the recovery process, they can be taught how to connect with others—starting exactly where they are and advancing forward one small step at a time.

Before I leave this topic of parents who set their children on paths of anxiety, intimacy problems, and limitation, listen to this.

Parents don't have to pass on this intergenerational angst any longer. They can be taught how to respond to their babies in ways that enhance security.

In a study by van den Boom in the Netherlands, mothers were helped to learn how to interpret infant cries and were taught to respond to the whole range of infant signals.[23]

Without training, mothers in this study ignored or responded ineffectively to mild cues of their babies' discomfort such as fussing; interfered with or ignored infant exploration; and ignored positive efforts their children made toward attachment, such as smiling, reaching, or trying to be close. Children were generally responded to only after they sent negative signals, such as prolonged crying.

Through intervention and coaching, these mothers learned to respond positively when their children did something positive. They learned to be attentive to their children's exploration without interfering in it.

The good news is that we can all learn how to create secure, joyous children.

But what about for misery addicts? Since it's too late to crawl back into the womb and start over, what can you do? For starters, you can find a recovery community. I'll discuss this more thoroughly in chapter 20, but in the meantime, let this stew in your pot: whether you believe it now or not, recovery groups are filled with people just like you.

CHAPTER SIXTEEN

Evicting a Source of Good

Kali Rose, her thinking distorted by days of too little sleep, too many cigarettes, and inadequate nutrition—all a consequence of abandoning her recovery meetings and staying with a very critical relative—planned to make a solitary retreat at her therapist's retreat house and forgot one thing: to reserve the house.

Consequently, when she went to the house when no one was there and she wasn't expected, she couldn't find the key. She was outraged. She'd gone to all the trouble of going to the house, and now she couldn't get in.

She responded with many calls to the manager and so many calls to her therapist that she used up the answering machine's memory. Then she accused her therapist of refusing to pick up the phone—as if the therapist could know it was her calling—forgetting that her therapist never left the ringer on so as to not disturb client sessions.

Then she created a reason to miss her therapy group, sending the message through another group member, with a comment about the therapist's answering machine not working—neglecting to realize that the machine's brain was tied up with her own messages.

This demonstrates a classic cascade of setups that typifies a misery addict in a flare-up of the disorder.

The messages she left were reiterations of how other people should have done this and should have done that, with many of the same comments repeated several times. What was missing was taking any responsibility for her own role. She also failed to notice or acknowledge that the same thing had happened just weeks before, and she had been told exactly what to do so it wouldn't happen again. The series of comments to her therapist had a battering energy to them. It was as if she were hitting her therapist with a certain set of words over and over. Through the years, she had done this with the therapist—deluged her with words and pummeling energy—whenever she was seriously displeased. Her therapist was wearing out.

As we've seen before, from a psychological perspective, Kali Rose's behavior was understandable. She's furious at a mother she can't be angry at, so she needs stand-ins. The people she elects to this position are usually women she admires and who can help her. Eventually she alienates these women. As insecure children do, she absorbed her father's defense of ragefulness and used it against herself and others, though not physically or with directly rageful words.

The tragedy of untreated misery addiction is that misery addicts have trouble spotting or remembering their own destructive patterns, and often they are powerless over stopping them, even if they are conscious of them.

In the heat of her rage, Kali Rose lost all consciousness of the effect she was having on her relationships. She had something she had to say. She had to say it again and again. Her need obscured the consequences.

When people have no consciousness of the effect they are having on others (assuming their minds aren't under the influence of some drug), they have tapped into a very young state. Babies and toddlers don't have the capacity to discern their impact on others. Still Kali Rose is an adult, so she's responsible for the impact of her actions, even when her needs overrule her ability to realize what she's doing.

It's not okay to batter someone with words, even when that person is your therapist. Her therapist had to set a limit. Kali Rose was now at risk of losing the person who held open the door to a different way of life.

Should Kali Rose lose her therapist, she will enter another phase of her pattern: she is often unable to effectively use a benefit until the deadline for it has passed.

For example, Kali Rose requested that a teacher leave lecture materials for her to copy. The teacher left them for her for three months. When it was time to gather them up, she gave Kali Rose two weeks' notice. A week after they were put away, Kali Rose called and asked for them.

She repeated this pattern throughout treatment. Kali Rose had missed many days of treatment and missed many days that were available for her to stay at the retreat house. A few weeks before the end of the program she said, "I wish I could live there now." She could have been living there for months, but she only felt ready to do it when it was too late.

For her therapist, it was sad. She watched as good was handed to Kali Rose on a platter, but Kali Rose kept her head turned until the platter was being put back in the cupboard. Then she said, "Wait, I want that now."

This pattern is no mystery. It acts out precisely what happened to Kali Rose in her infancy. When she was two years old, her mother created a deadline. That was the point at which Kali Rose's mother abandoned her in order to focus on her angry husband. She handed Kali Rose a metaphorical pink slip that said, "Nurturing parenting is now over." And all her life, Kali Rose has been saying, "Wait, I want that now. I want you to extend the deadline."

Every time she loses a friend or a beloved mentor, she says, "I want you to extend the deadline." Every time she misses a due date, she says, "I want you to extend the deadline." Every cell in her being wants to go back to two years and two minutes old and for that deadline to disappear. She didn't have her mom for nearly long enough, so no amount of time with a person or a task is ever long enough.

The patterns that produce misery addiction are powerful. They are a person's issues writ large. This particular pattern—of pushing away good, of missing opportunities, and of wearing out the people who can offer deliverance—is the saddest of all.

There's an escape hatch from the tyranny of childhood patterns. A misery addict tends to close it.

CHAPTER SEVENTEEN

Self-Sabotage

We come at last to the primary behavior of misery addiction: self-sabotage.

With other addictions, the tool that enacts or sustains the addiction is obvious. An alcoholic seeks a change in mood; the tool is alcohol; the addiction is to alcohol. A drug addict seeks a change in his mood or mental state; the tool is a drug; the addiction is to the drug. A food addict seeks a change in alertness and mood; the tool is food; the addiction is to food.

With misery addiction, the addiction is to an antiquated survival system; the state sought is avoidance and nonalertness; the tool used is self-sabotage.

Self-sabotage is an action (or nonaction) on the misery addict's part that leads to a negative consequence for her. It can be as simple as not putting new toilet paper within reach near the end of the roll or letting the newspapers pile up until the pile is overwhelming. It can also result from a series of behaviors so complex that the addict's part in bringing about the negative result is invisible.

One way to spot self-sabotage is that the proportions are off between the initiating action (or nonaction) and the consequences. Characteristically the initiating action (or nonaction) is far easier or more bearable than the consequence. A relatively severe, punitive, or time-consuming consequence could have been prevented by a relatively simple, time-efficient measure.

Remember the situation with Sammie being late for her walk with Voula? Even though Voula set a time limit, Sammie's lateness continued. Finally Voula said, "I can't stand the tension of waiting for you. I'm starting to get nervous when I get ready to meet you. I realized I'd developed these waiting strategies. I'd take a book. I'd take my junk mail. I'd try to estimate how late you'd be and then tuck in a trip to the bank, but then I'd be rushed because I didn't want to be later than you, so then I'd feel frazzled as I pushed through traffic to get to you. It's not the way I want to arrange my day. Plus I feel that my time is not respected. I'm getting near a limit here. I need you to be on time."

"When was I late?" Sammie asked.

Voula looked at her. "I can't believe you are asking me that question. You are late all the time."

"For example?"

Voula blew air through her bangs. "Okay, you were late when we were going to see *The Pianist* together."

"I called you," said Sammie.

"Yes, but by then I'd already been waiting outside and watching the line grow. By the time I got in the theater, I had to sit too far forward. Then I couldn't relax because I kept looking for you, worried that you wouldn't be able to find me. Plus I felt guilty saving a seat when the place was packed and people kept asking me if the seat was taken. So instead of being able to take in the beginning of the movie, I kept looking for you."

"I brought you popcorn to make up for it."

"Sammie, you aren't getting it. It changed the whole experience because you were late. Think about how it would have been if you'd been on time. We'd have met and been happy to see each other. We'd have gone in together. One of us would get good seats while the other got popcorn. We'd chat and catch up before it started. Then we'd both be sharing the experience of the movie from the beginning. We'd also have had better seats."

"Okay, I see that."

"So I'm saying our friendship rests on this. I've reached my limit. Don't be late again."

"What if I can't help it? Don't I get a grace period?"

"I don't have it in me. I can't go through this anymore."

"It's not fair to not give me a grace period."

"Maybe it isn't. But I don't have it in me."

"Well, I'll never be late again. I promise."

The next time they arranged to meet for dinner, Sammie was late. Voula waited forty-five minutes for Sammie to arrive. She was so angry that she didn't order, and when Sammie came in, she said, "This is it, Sammie. I'm leaving."

"How can you leave? I couldn't help it. There was an accident on the interstate and traffic was snarled. I was sure I could get here in thirty minutes. I left thirty-five minutes before our meeting time. I didn't think there'd be any problem. It's the middle of the day. The interstate is usually easy midday."

"You gave yourself a five-minute buffer when you knew our friendship rested on you being on time? Five minutes? And this is based on the interstate being clear when the interstate is unpredictable?"

"I thought that would be plenty of time."

"Sammie, answer me this. As important as this was, what kept you from being sure you weren't taking any chances?"

"I thought it would be plenty of time."

"What kept you from thinking about the consequences if it wasn't?"

"I don't know."

"Okay. Bye."

"You're still leaving?"

"I said I'd reached my limit. I was so angry sitting here I almost didn't wait for you."

"I couldn't help it."

"You could help it, Sammie. I was here. I came by the same interstate. But it was important to me and I didn't want to take any chances, so I left forty-five minutes early, enough time to get here by surface roads if the interstate got clogged. I was so sure you'd be on time that I didn't want to take any chance that I'd be late. I'm done here. I just can't do this anymore."

This is what gives the appearance to outsiders that Sammie wants to be miserable. Prevention of the negative outcome seems easy in contrast to the result, which can cost a lot.

SABOTAGE AS A LIFESTYLE

When we ran our first retreat program for misery addiction, I naively thought that once the clients were in a safe place with all their needs abundantly provided for, they would embrace recovery and therapy. I was astounded at the variety of ways people created to sabotage themselves. They arrived too late for orientation, lost notebooks, didn't read the list of things to bring, read the list and still didn't bring the things they needed, showed up late to sessions, tried to skip meals, weren't ready when it was time to start or stop an exercise, created issues that sidetracked the main process, gave away their talking time in the group, set themselves up to be rejected by others, did all the chores, did none of the chores, stayed up too late, stayed too linked to people at home through excessive phone calls, took so long in the bathroom that others got resentful, used the computer after hours, and volunteered but didn't follow through. The sheer variety, ingenuity, and subtlety of the many forms of self-sabotage impressed me.

Nora, for example, tended to stay quiet and let everyone else go first so that by the time she took her turn, everyone's energy was used up and the group session was nearly over. (This replicated her childhood experience of being born after her parents got tired of parenting.) She was the first to jump up and volunteer to help in the kitchen. She was the one at the dishwasher, helping rinse the dishes. It could be easy to miss that she was avoiding herself (her primary strategy) by sacrificing herself for others (her primary tool).

Self-sabotage for a misery addict is not just a bad habit; it's a way of living. We say to alcoholics in treatment, "It doesn't matter what your reasons for starting to drink were. Now you have a problem on its own—your addiction to alcohol." The same is true for misery addicts. They have compelling, heartrending reasons for developing this strategy for survival. And now they have another problem—a way of life that is built around self-sabotage.

Amala's mom, Jo, was mean-spirited. She couldn't stand for Amala to accomplish anything or be happy. Whenever Amala visited her mom, Jo would squelch her joy and put her down in some way. When Amala felt good about joining an exercise club and getting fit, her mom said she was vain. That soured Amala's joy in taking care of herself. She stopped going to the club. Amala got promoted at her job, and her mom said she was getting above herself.

Others encouraged Amala to keep any joyful news from her mother. But Amala couldn't do it. She'd always run to her mom with her latest accomplishment and then have the juice taken out.

Long after quitting smoking, we can pat our pockets for a cigarette in a moment of stress. There's a reason some Alano clubs (houses where alcoholics have meetings and a social center) have the ambience of a bar even though no alcohol is served. The constellation of behaviors around our addiction becomes a natural part of us.

In misery addiction the associated behaviors are part of the addiction. Instead of one clear-cut, obvious action—such as picking up a bottle and drinking—a misery addict has a repertoire of harmful behaviors he is loyal to, some of which can be quite subtle.

Kali Rose had one that was really difficult to see. She would volunteer to do something for her circle of friends. It would be very involved and would take a lot of time. It was such a grand offer that the others were thrilled. It's something they wouldn't have thought of wanting if she hadn't offered. At first everyone, including Kali Rose, glowed because of her lovely idea and their pleasure in it.

But for Kali Rose that glow soon turned into a feeling of pressure. The reality was that she was already preoccupied with pressing demands from her work and her family. She didn't have time to do the project. So it hung over her head, getting heavier by the day. Eventually she realized she simply wasn't able to do it and will continue to punish herself long after for not completing it.

Meanwhile the people she promised started feeling confused. They ended up being set up themselves, because they loved Kali Rose's idea, and then they were puzzled at the long span of time during which there was no word about it. When Kali Rose finally said she couldn't do it, they were forgiving. Since it was all voluntary on Kali Rose's part, they felt they had to repress their irritation at her having broken a promise. But their repressed irritation inserted some distance into their friendship.

The choreography of sabotage can be so automatic and subtle that the person creating it may not be conscious that a single slight action will lead to a disruptive outcome.

Some characteristics of misery addiction are standard to any addiction. These include a desperate need to be in control (looking controlling from the outside or controlling by abdicating), poor anger management skills (either raging or suppressing anger), impulse problems (usually alternating impulsiveness with excessive control), crossing one's own moral boundaries (thinking oneself honest but lying and manipulating others to support the addiction), being stuck in repetitive behaviors that continue not to work, returning to places or people that support the addiction, financial problems, problems with intimacy (loss of friends, sequential intimacies), and a tendency to isolate oneself.

Not all addicts, and not all misery addicts, do every item in the above paragraph, but nearly all have experienced most of these situations over time.

THE MAZE HAS A PATTERN

An addiction to misery, unlike more obvious addictions such as food and alcohol addiction, can wear many masks. The way it looks on Ingrid is very different from the way it manifests for Helena. This can make it difficult to spot in friends and a challenge to discover in oneself.

To find it, look for the pattern. A misery addict has a pattern of making choices and responding to situations in a way that keeps her from joy and fulfillment. The underlying system by which each person does this varies. Yet in common is the missed path, the absence of belief in one's own potential for attracting and keeping good things, and the sense of waiting for death (or something else beyond the person's control) to resolve the problem.

See if you can detect the pattern in the following examples:

Mattie was great with radio quiz shows. She won a trip for two to Hawaii, gift certificates galore, free dinners at fancy restaurants, and a raft of movie tickets. The hitch? She never used them. She collected the certificates or vouchers and stuck them in a drawer.

When she changed jobs, she left early, missing her going-away party.

She loved to garden. She grew a variety of vegetables. Most rotted on the vine.

What's the pattern?

Mattie does the work but doesn't let herself have the benefit. She deprives herself of the celebration, the reward.

– Exercise 3: Ten Troubles –

Now it's time to look at yourself and look for your own pattern. A single experience will take on more meaning as you find similarities with other experiences. If you step back far enough, you may be able to see a theme in your actions and choices. Read the following questions and write down your answers in a notebook or on your computer.

1. List ten unhappy outcomes that you've experienced recently.
2. Study the list. What commonalities can you detect among these experiences?
3. Is there something you did in each case that contributed to the outcome, something you could easily (or relatively easily) have done differently, or not done at all?
4. Is there something in common among them that you *didn't* do—and that you could have done relatively easily—that contributed to the unhappy outcome?
5. Can you put the common elements together and see a theme?

– Exercise 4: Knot My Problem –

Take a piece of yarn, twine, or string. Carry it with you all day. Every time you do something that sabotages good for you, put a knot in your string.

At the end of the day, talk to someone about each knot.

- Try carrying a new string each day for a week.
- Try writing a list of all the knot-causing events at the end of each day.
- Study your list at the end of the week to look for patterns.
- Consider sharing your list with someone else to get a fresh perspective on your patterns.

CHAPTER EIGHTEEN

Symptoms

The following list pulls together various aspects of misery addiction, many of which have been discussed in previous chapters:

- having a pattern of self-sabotage
- being avoidant
- losing track of the main objective
- injecting negatives into positive situations
- leaving or stopping a positive chain of events
- having a fear of well-being, happiness, or success
- not acting when action is required
- being indecisive
- being ambivalent
- longing for a certain experience but insisting that it take a form that can't or doesn't work
- insisting that the first steps toward a goal take a certain form
- wanting something you'll never get if you keep doing what you're doing
- feeling that your life is jinxed
- feeling that you're incompetent or unworthy
- not changing your behavior even after it repeatedly causes problems
- after discovering a pattern, not adjusting to deal with it

- acting on assumptions without checking them out first
- being resistant
- always having an excuse (yes, but)
- splitting hairs
- refusing helpful medication
- isolating
- resist asking for or receiving help
- alienating the people who can offer the most help or do the most good
- sacrificing
- being attracted to unavailable people
- feeling that you can never fit in or belong
- craving closeness but evading intimacy
- having multiple addictions or compulsive behaviors

All of us do some of these things from time to time, and not every misery addict will do everything on the list. What differentiates a misery addict is that she is locked into a pattern of many of these attitudes and actions. As a result, progress toward realizing her goals is blocked, and a significant portion of her daily experience is unsatisfying. A misery addict is rarely content—numbed, maybe, through the use of a tool addiction, but not content, rarely or never resting in moments of quietude and serenity.

Let's go back through the items on this list, one by one, in more detail. For items that have already been described in detail in previous chapters, I will give but a brief comment and/or an example or two. New symptoms will be explained more thoroughly.

HAVING A PATTERN OF SELF-SABOTAGE

This consists of recurrent actions (or nonactions) that lead to negative consequences—consequences that are often disproportionately costly or painful.

BEING AVOIDANT

Examples of avoidant behavior are not stepping all the way into experiences, intimacy, or feelings—not being fully present to life.

LOSING TRACK OF THE MAIN OBJECTIVE

Allie wanted to be promoted at her job. She knew her odds would improve if she studied the new program material and could show familiarity with it. Also, some good friends told her she needed to dress differently to look more professional. She decided to go to the mall and use her recent paycheck to remodel her wardrobe. Then she planned to spend the weekend studying the new program.

She went shopping, but on the way to the clothing store, she got sidetracked into a gadget store and bought a fancy ice-cream maker and a little robot that carried things, using up most of her paycheck.

She decided to go to a consignment shop to see if she could find something affordable. Once there, she saw all these cute clothes for her niece, which she bought, cleaning out her wallet.

Allie's plan got sidetracked by tool addictions. Impulsive shopping, sacrificing, compulsive spending, and busyness—all are avoidant activities. She avoided herself right out of the actions that would have supported her promotion.

Misery addicts with attention deficit disorder (ADD) are especially vulnerable to getting sidetracked. However, once ADD is diagnosed, simple tools can be used to keep their brains on track.

A misery addict with ADD will be resistant to using these tools, even though they work. He may lose track of the stated goal because of a *hidden,* more powerful main objective: to prevent the discomfort of success. His system creates shifting daily objectives, all designed for immediate avoidance—and all leading to predictable distress.

INJECTING NEGATIVES INTO POSITIVE SITUATIONS

Kenneth took his wife out for their anniversary. He assumed that, since it was a Thursday, the popular restaurant he'd selected would have tables available. Standing with his wife at the maître d's desk, he discovered his assumption was incorrect. With the slight effort of a phone call, he could have ensured a special occasion that would have enhanced his bond with his wife.

Elva was supposed to bring rolls to the Thanksgiving dinner at her sister's house. Though some folks would rejoice at a gift of pick-led squid, it's not that great at sopping gravy. By not bringing what her sister requested, Elva set up annoyance from her sister, who then had to paw through the freezer hunting for bread at the very time she wanted to be mashing potatoes.

At the table, everyone was in a holiday mood, laughing at jokes and telling old family stories. As her father entered with a platter laden with a golden roasted turkey, Elva interrupted the oohing by telling the story of how some turkey farms operate. The mood crashed, of course, and everyone was at a loss. The meal began in silence and discomfort, no one knowing how to save the occasion, and her sister was in tears that, after all the work she had done, the anticipated joy of her family gathering was lost.

LEAVING OR STOPPING A POSITIVE CHAIN OF EVENTS

Elliot had to drag through each day. He began to consider that his low energy level was due to his poor eating habits. He heard that eating healthy foods does a body good. (It's not exactly breaking news, but when we're ready, our ears open.) He thought he should add a simple breakfast of a bit of protein and a bit of fruit each morning instead of his usual coffee and carbo on the run, plus maybe something green for lunch.

At the store, though, he wandered down those inner aisles and got lots of food that comes in boxes. He resolved to have a sit-down breakfast each morning, but he kept getting up too late for that. At work he only had time to get lunch out of a machine. For dinner he did a drive-thru.

Finally he decided to spend a few days at a spa with a food and exercise program to get himself started. He did well there. His en-ergy shot up. He walked every day. His mind was clearer. He felt stronger. But back home after the spa, he went right back to his old methods. Being alert was not that comfortable.

Life is full of chain reactions. By going to bed early, it's easier to rise in time to have breakfast, gather your thoughts, meditate, and exercise before going to work. By going to night school, you gradually gather the credentials that put you closer to the job you really want.

Discover and pursue one of your passions and your life gets richer. You meet like-minded folks. You expose yourself to a new friendship pool, and you feel better about yourself. You put yourself in the vicinity of serendipity.

When you're addicted to misery, it's difficult to get into—or stay in—a positive chain reaction. Things get in the way of getting started. Things happen that cause you to abandon the steps that are leading to a happier place. Or the improved circumstances feel foreign, and you take a spiral staircase back down to the basement.

HAVING A FEAR OF WELL-BEING, HAPPINESS, OR SUCCESS

Amy struggled for years to become a college professor, gathering credentials, teaching 8:00 A.M. classes, and surviving the tenure process. Now, at last, she had made it. She was teaching classes she liked. She was respected by her colleagues. Then she won a poetry award that gave her academic acclaim and made her name known at faculty gatherings.

Yet it made her nervous. She wasn't used to things going well. She was used to struggling. She wasn't accustomed to actually having arrived at the end of the struggle.

Instead of an increasing feeling of well-being, Amy felt dread building. She was nervously waiting for the shoe to drop. The danger is that she may *cause* the shoe to drop in order to break the suspense. She may even design and build the shoe.

She lives inside the terrible paradox of misery addiction, unable to enjoy positive events and feeling more comfortable with struggle. From that position, it can feel better to stop the flow of goodness than to wait in suspense for someone else to do it.

NOT ACTING WHEN ACTION IS REQUIRED

When Samantha was offered a chance to represent her company at the national convention in Chicago—both an honor and a perk—she froze. She thought of a million reasons why she shouldn't go.

She didn't deserve it. Colleagues would envy her, and therefore resent her, and therefore sabotage her. The cat would miss her. She hadn't been east of the Rockies before. Big cities scared her.

Turning it down would feel safer, more comfortable, more routine. It would also take her out of the running for the A-list. To refuse the company's vote of confidence would cause a shift in attitude that would alter the opportunities presented to her in the future.

She took a long time to decide. Her hesitation was in itself a message to her company.

Delaying or not acting when action is needed is a classic symptom of misery addiction.

BEING INDECISIVE

The misery addict waffles back and forth, losing a lot of time and missing opportunities through a failure to decide.

BEING AMBIVALENT

She wants intimacy. She fears it.

He wants to marry Suzanne. He's scared of the idea of marriage.

LONGING FOR A CERTAIN EXPERIENCE BUT INSISTING THAT IT TAKE A FORM THAT CAN'T OR DOESN'T WORK

Patrice longed to explore Europe in a leisurely fashion with the man of her dreams. The problem was, the men who kept appearing were far from her dream.

After hearing Patrice complain about this in the lunchroom at work, a coworker, Senya, with whom Patrice had always gotten along well, piped up, "I've always wanted to explore Europe that way. That's one of my big dreams. Perhaps you and I could do that. I'd really like to get together with you and talk about it."

"Sure," Patrice responded without enthusiasm, not for a minute planning to follow up.

Patrice wanted to do this with a man or not at all.

If you want something very, very badly, you need to think outside the box. Allow your mind to broaden and invite others to brainstorm with you.

However, a misery addict is likely to find objections to any new ideas and to keep himself from pursuing alternate possibilities—thus obstructing his own joy through a closed mind.

INSISTING THAT THE FIRST STEPS TOWARD A GOAL TAKE A CERTAIN FORM

Marla wanted to get married. She dated lots of eligible guys, some of whom were very interested in her. But she'd always wanted to marry a farmer. If a guy wasn't a farmer, she wasn't interested. It would have helped her chances if she'd moved to farm country and mixed in the circles at the Grange and co-op, but she kept looking for her farmer in downtown Seattle. Eventually one nice guy began falling for her. He was willing to move to the country, get chickens, and make a big garden for her. But she turned away because that wasn't truly farming.

Not all of our opportunities arrive in a tuxedo with an engraved invitation. Sometimes first options look pretty scruffy. The path toward our heartfelt goals may meander in some odd directions at first. But if we are alert, open, and broad-minded, we can feel it when an option is in the ballpark and take it on the chance that it will get us where we want to go.

WANTING SOMETHING YOU'LL NEVER GET IF YOU KEEP DOING WHAT YOU'RE DOING

This is a corollary to the previous two. Odette wanted to become a massage therapist. Two good schools were within a reasonable distance and both had extended-payment programs and evening curricula. She could afford to go if she stopped shopping compulsively and if she quit using up her evenings hanging out at a favorite neighborhood bar.

Odette wasn't even a drinker. Going to school wouldn't take her away from the bar completely; she could always go on the three nights a week when there was no class. But she couldn't tear herself away. It was her secure base, and stepping toward her dream represented risk.

FEELING THAT YOUR LIFE IS JINXED

Charlie said, "I believe other people can have what they dream of. I just don't believe I can. The only thing I've ever wanted was to be a doctor. But what's the use of even trying for it? I don't have what it takes.

"I tried to make myself into a sales rep, but I can't do it. It doesn't feel right to me to talk people into buying what they can't afford and don't need. Then I tried to learn computer programming, but machines leave me cold.

"You want to know what I really think? Deep down, I don't believe I have the potential, the raw material that would let me get what I want. You could say I'm in mourning for that all of the time."

FEELING THAT YOU'RE INCOMPETENT OR UNWORTHY

Remedios yearned to have children. Just the sound of a child's laughter pierced her heart with longing. She was the favorite "auntie" of all her friends' children. She liked nothing better than sitting on the floor at her brother's house, reading her nieces a story while they sprawled across her lap.

She didn't want to be a single parent, but she hadn't found a man who seemed like true husband/father material.

Actually, the problem went deeper. In her heart she felt unworthy of having her truest desires fulfilled.

This sense of unworthiness dictated her behavior in subtle ways so that she turned away from men who had the potential of being good dads. She thwarted the interactions that could have led to her joy.

NOT CHANGING YOUR BEHAVIOR EVEN AFTER IT
REPEATEDLY CAUSES PROBLEMS

Serena had a penchant for locking herself out of the house. The obvious (and common) solution was to plant extra keys in various spots. But Serena had to lock herself out nine times before she finally had spare keys made.

AFTER DISCOVERING A PATTERN,
NOT ADJUSTING TO DEAL WITH IT

In fact, after Serena locked herself out for the fifth time, her husband noticed that she did this when she was stressed and told her so. Once she knew the pattern, then she had an opportunity to create a plan around it.

But a misery addict often doesn't adjust, even when the handwriting is clearly visible on the wall. Thus she sets herself up to go through the negative experience yet again.

ACTING ON ASSUMPTIONS WITHOUT
CHECKING THEM OUT FIRST

Wilt would get an idea in his head and then proceed as if the idea were a fact. He never questioned or checked to see if his idea was a reality. It drove his wife crazy.

He'd assume his wife was angry with him and then be cold to her, never checking to see if in fact she was. He'd assume she'd pack the fishing poles for vacation and never ask her to, even though he was the one who wanted to fish and she had a lot to do just packing the kitchen items and the kids.

He'd assume a store would still be open at 8:00, not call, and then get there too late to pick up the prescription. He'd assume a friend would make the first move for having lunch together and wait . . . and wait. Then, when the friend didn't call, he'd be hurt and decide the friend didn't like him. He didn't check to see if the friend was just busy and needed him to be the one to set up the lunch date this time around.

BEING RESISTANT

He wants his life to change but resists the therapist's efforts.

She wants to join the inner circle of the Weaver's Club but resists overtures of inclusion.

ALWAYS HAVING AN EXCUSE (YES, BUT)

Stanford was tired of being a fisherman. The money wasn't as good now that the fish stocks were shrinking. He was tired of the cold and the wet. He was weary of leaving home for months at a time. Yet he didn't know what else to do for a living.

He was resourceful, a hard worker, a quick learner, personable, educated (he had a B.A. in history). He was employable.

His friends had ideas.

"Yes, but . . . "

His friends had offers.

"Yes, but . . . "

Sometimes a misery addict will feel some satisfaction in saying that nothing can work. Listing all the things that went wrong or all the people who failed him can be a way to feel special.

SPLITTING HAIRS

Moe won tickets to the semifinals and asked his friend Joe to join him, knowing Joe loved basketball.

"What day is the game?"

"Thursday."

"I guess I can go. How early are you planning to go?"

"About 6:00."

"Well, I usually eat dinner at 6:00, but I guess I could get something there. How were you planning to get there?"

Moe, getting irritated, said, "I'm driving to the park and ride and taking the special bus."

"Won't that take longer?"

Moe clipped his words, "Afterward, it will be faster. All the traffic leaving the stadium at once will cause a jam. The buses line up at the door and whisk us away."

"Where are the seats?"

"Joe, forget it. I thought I was offering you a special opportunity."

"No, no, I want to go. Thanks."

Unless Joe reveals some special social quality at the game, Joe just got his last invitation from Moe. By getting lost in logistical details and not appreciating the big picture—that a friend had offered him something special—he killed his friend's generous impulse.

REFUSING HELPFUL MEDICATION

Here is one of the definitive symptoms of misery addiction: the person is depressed; medication helps her; yet she stops taking it. She goes through this cycle again and again. This is because a misery addict is uncomfortable with a stable, positive mood.

Sometimes people reject antidepressants because certain brands lower sex drive. However, not all antidepressants have that effect. And even if they did, compare the following lists of pros and cons:

Pros:
  feel better
  have more energy
  get more done
  make better choices
  more receptive to social opportunities
  more likely to advance at work
  eat better
  get along better with others
  live a more organized life
  keep up with everyday tasks (balancing the checkbook, doing
      the laundry, sending birthday cards to friends, and so on)

Cons:
  less sexual interest

It makes sense that a person addicted to misery would not want to stay on antidepressants. The drugs help too much. Feeling better increases the tension that comes from things going too well.

ISOLATING

A misery addict feels alone in the world. He may be the life of the party, but he is crying inside. Purposely or inadvertently, he does things that create a barrier or distance from others.

RESIST ASKING FOR OR RECEIVING HELP

A misery addict will sweat through an overwhelming task rather than ask for help. When help is offered, she is likely to turn it down, even if it is desperately needed.

ALIENATING THE PEOPLE WHO CAN OFFER THE MOST HELP OR DO THE MOST GOOD

The misery addict wears out or alienates his therapist. He gets kicked out of the recovery program. He acts inappropriately toward his boss.

SACRIFICING

The misery addict may give too much of herself to others, often at her own expense.

BEING ATTRACTED TO UNAVAILABLE PEOPLE

Caron loved her husband, but she was miserable in her marriage. Occasionally Thaddeus would be thoughtful. This was the exception though; most of the time, Thad was preoccupied with his own concerns. He put his money toward his own passions, and he always had a reason why Caron's needs for attention or money should stay on the back burner.

Caron felt entirely alone in her marriage. Every day, Thaddeus did or said twenty thoughtless things that sent Caron the message that she was not in his thoughts or his heart.

Caron's energy level slowly dropped. Her belief in herself waned. Her ability to risk decreased. She got sick more often.

Her friend Sylvia was disgusted with Thad's lack of investment in Caron, and she urged Caron to leave. Caron argued, "He doesn't beat me. He's a good provider. And just last year he bought me a sweater."

FEELING THAT YOU CAN NEVER FIT IN OR BELONG

Eadan entered college with solid academic credentials, a quick mind, and limited social experience. She didn't understand that there are unwritten rules about the actions that attract and sustain friendships or that certain conduct shoos people away. Her lack of social skills caused her to lose some potential friends whom she liked very much and left her clinging to other folks who exploited her naïveté. She wasn't entirely comfortable with that circle, but it was better than not having any circle at all. Still, over time, her unskilled behavior caused her to lose this group of people as well.

By the time she received her graduate degree, her social world was narrow. She decided she was meant to be an outsider and destined to stay that way. She told herself that she wasn't going to belong to any inner circle, so she gave up on the possibility, pulling a tight shield around herself that was as good as a prison.

The truth, of course, is that relationships aren't magic but a result of intelligent choosing and deliberate actions, all of which can be studied and practiced and learned (though not painlessly).

A misery addict, however, would have great difficulty in taking the first step to change the situation—for example, signing up for a workshop that develops these skills.

CRAVING CLOSENESS BUT EVADING INTIMACY

This is the paradox that causes the most pain for those addicted to misery—and also for the people who love them.

Sverno loved his wife, Natasha—at a distance. He liked the idea of her. He loved reading the paper and hearing her humming as she potted plants nearby. He liked her presence in the house and in his life—except when she tried to get close.

After lovemaking she'd want to cuddle near him, and he would feel suffocated and make some excuse to get up. She touched him as he ate breakfast, and he flinched away from her. She wanted to celebrate their anniversary, but when she stared at him lovingly across a candlelit table, he couldn't stop himself from saying something mean, to get her to back off. Sometimes he'd start a fight just to get her to leave the room.

Susan had a different twist on evading intimacy. She found lots of men to love, and most loved her back. But they all happened to be married. With one exception: she fell hard for a parish priest.

Sverno sabotaged intimacy within his marriage. Susan never got to home plate.

A misery addict has a penchant for being attracted to unavailable people, people who are safe to want or love because they'll never create the risk of fulfilled intimacy. Such an attraction offers pseudo-intimacy.

HAVING MULTIPLE ADDICTIONS
OR COMPULSIVE ACTIVITIES

Involvement in a mixture of activities such as compulsive gambling, shopping, eating, or game-playing and/or use of various substances to alter mood or feeling serve the triple purpose of checking out, soothing pain, and causing more misery.

Everyone screws up now and then and loses an opportunity. All of us get distracted from our main goal on occasion. But when such things happen in a pattern, either cyclically or routinely, there's a problem.

YOUR CHOICE

One of my clients was recently criticizing herself for the years she had lost to indecision, inaction, or mistakes. In fact, she has lost many years due to criticizing herself. Clearly, each new year of self-judging causes her to lose another year. If her goal is to be endlessly angry with herself, then she will succeed, because this is working. Meanwhile, life continues to pass her by.

I asked her if four years from now, when she will be sixty, will she want to look back on four years of interesting activities or on sixty years of feeling like a failure? She smiled in recognition. Even though she is comfortable with defeat, she has worked hard enough therapeutically that she was able to honestly say that she wanted to look back on four good years.

This is your decision now. Is it worth it to you to work hard— sometimes very hard—for a few years so that you can feel joy as joy and so that happiness makes you happy? Would you like to have a real say in the course your life takes?

If your answer is yes but you feel scared, that's okay. It's okay to be scared at the prospect of happiness. Everyone gets scared at first by the prospect of big change, even if it's positive.

The rest of this book is about how to navigate these new and uncharted waters, about living a life that's truly fulfilling.

PART TWO

Finding and Living the Solution

CHAPTER NINETEEN

A Look in the Mirror

An alcoholic is an alcoholic, period. Once you're over the line into true alcohol addiction, you can't be a partial or some-of-the-time alcoholic.

The number of smokers who can take or leave nicotine is slim indeed. Most of us who have smoked (including me and many other people who have successfully quit) found a ferocious struggle in escaping the addiction.

Misery addiction, in contrast, falls along a continuum. On the far end are misery addicts who have seriously curtailed their lives and are unable to stop themselves from ongoing sabotage. On the other end are people who keep themselves a little bit unhappy—not actually staying miserable, but shying away from fulfillment. The amount of effort required to begin recovering from a misery addiction is determined in part by your place on the continuum.

So first, I'd like you to measure the degree of your own attachment to misery. Read the descriptions that follow; then mark where you feel you are on the continuum on page 137.

YOU EMBRACE LIFE

You embrace the joys of life. You let yourself feel the full range of emotions. You are fully present during lovemaking. You make positive choices for yourself. You take good care of your physical

needs. When you know what you want, you will arrange a respect-
ful and fair way to get it, if possible. You respect your own process
of thinking, living, and making decisions. You are optimistic.

YOU'RE MILDLY AVOIDANT

You've let yourself have much of what life has to offer, but there are
times when you keep yourself a bit removed. You might be a little
distracted during lovemaking. You keep a thin veil between yourself
and some experiences so that you are dampening the full impact of
all-out joy or all-out grief. You almost relax on vacations.

You take pretty good care of yourself physically. You sometimes
drink, eat, or do a little too much, but you can also stop yourself
from getting drunk or too full. You overwork at times, but then
you cut back to be with your friends or family. You know what
matters to you, and though it can sometimes take you a little while
to actually start toward a goal, you do get started, and then you
keep going until you get there, with few side trips.

YOU'RE AVOIDANT

You have good in your life, but there are certain aspects of your
life that are unhappy. It's difficult for you to let yourself be fully
present in joyful experiences. At a birthday party where you are
the guest of honor, or during lovemaking, or on a holiday, your attention might be more on other people or things than on yourself.
You wrestle with at least one addiction or compulsion; if you're in
recovery from it, your efforts proceed in fits and starts. You know
what you want to be doing in life, and you sort of do it sometimes,
but you haven't let yourself pursue it full tilt.

YOU SABOTAGE YOURSELF

Your life is not happy. You tend to miss opportunities, either by not
seeing them or by delaying action to the point that they pass you
by. You have turned to addictive substances or practices to soothe
your indecision and sadness. You are underemployed for your level
of talent. You are not pursuing your dreams, in part because you

don't believe that you can ever achieve them—or that you deserve fulfillment.

In some ways you don't take good care of yourself. You don't accept help easily, and you've been known to push help away.

YOU'RE MISERABLE

You are very underemployed, or doing a job you hate, or risking the job you like. You are so fearful of being disappointed that you don't want to take the risk of trying to get the things you want. Your relationship with one or both parents is likely to be difficult or disappointing. The relationships you have are unsatisfying. You tend to isolate yourself. It's difficult for you to trust others. You can't let yourself have very much help. You have a deep pool of anger that needs to be drained. Addictive substances or practices have helped you survive.

THE CONTINUUM

Mark your spot on the continuum below.

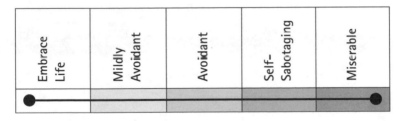

WHAT DO I NEED?

If you fall into the mildly avoidant category, you can change your life for the better just by reading this book and following its guidance. Most people in the middle category will also need the support of regular recovery meetings and/or the help of a good psychotherapist. If you are in the self-sabotaging or miserable categories, then in addition, I strongly recommend treatment for misery addiction, followed by a sustained, consistent recovery program and regular sessions with a good psychotherapist.

CHAPTER TWENTY

Recovery

Recovery is defined as getting back to normal or regaining what has been lost. For misery addicts (and other addicts too), recovery may actually bring experiences they've never had, such as kinship or self-confidence. In that sense, the term *recovery* is a misnomer. Nevertheless, it is the commonly used term that describes the process of rising from the depths of addiction and experiencing emancipation and joy.

Recovery offers community, sanity, and instruction on how to fully live.

For the sheer genius of the recovery process we can thank alcoholics. In 1935, two men known today simply as Dr. Bob and Bill W. began the process that led to the establishment of Alcoholics Anonymous. Since then, tens of millions of alcoholics all over the world have successfully followed their recipe for crawling out of addiction.

Over the past few decades, use of the Twelve Step process has spread to a growing list of other addictions and compulsive behaviors. It keeps working, no matter what type of problem it's applied to. It is effective for any problem of living, large or small. Over time, it can bring about a complete overhaul in the way one approaches life.

It isn't enough just to read about the recovery process. It has to be worked, personally put into practice. There are things we must actively do to experience recovery. However, once the process starts working—which is usually with one's first efforts and first recovery group meetings—it has a mysterious force of its own, bringing forward gifts, insight, and serendipitous happenings.

It works in a way opposite to addiction. Whereas addiction takes from us, recovery gives to us. Addiction makes our lives unmanageable; recovery causes life to become more orderly. Things mysteriously go wrong for us when we're stuck in addiction. Things mysteriously improve with recovery.

Addiction	Recovery
Chaos	Order
Things go wrong	Things work out
Unconsciousness	Consciousness
Losses	Gifts
Blindness	Insight
Isolation	Friends and community

The starting place for recovery is at recovery meetings or in a form of addiction treatment. Twelve Step recovery meetings (those founded on the same principles as Alcoholics Anonymous) end in the word *anonymous,* such as Alcoholics Anonymous and Misery Addicts Anonymous. (Exceptions: Alateen and Al-Anon—sometimes spelled ALANON—which are Twelve Step programs for people who have a partner, spouse, parent, friend, or relative with an addiction.)

These meetings are always free, but someone will pass a basket for donations that are used to buy supplies, pay rent on the room, and contribute to the home office of that particular Anonymous group. Most people donate a dollar, but less is fine and none is okay too. There are no professional group leaders. Leadership is rotated among members, and a standard format is followed for each meeting. To go to a meeting, just show up. No reservation or appointment is needed. There are no requirements or application. You don't have to reveal any personal information, not even your last name. You do not have to sign in.

In contrast, treatment is a professionally managed experience of recovery led by one or more psychologists, counselors, social workers, or other professionals.

If you continue to live in your regular home while you're in a treatment program, that program is usually called an outpatient program. (The term is borrowed from our medical system.) If you stay in a hospital or hospital-affiliated facility during treatment, you're in an inpatient program. And if your treatment takes place at a retreat center or recovery center, it's usually called a residential treatment program. Most residential programs are put together by recovery professionals who have a dedication to recovery and the people who seek it. Treatment facilities differ widely in price and are relatively expensive. As with so many things in life, some are much better than others. Cost is not necessarily an indicator of effectiveness or value.

The advantage of treatment programs over recovery meetings is that they immerse you in the recovery experience and protect you from relapse during any withdrawal. I prefer nonprofit treatment programs because they only have to meet expenses; they don't have to turn a profit for owners or stakeholders.

Some treatment facilities run aftercare programs, which means they offer at least one weekly group meeting for alumni for a certain number of weeks after they've completed treatment.

However, no treatment program is sufficient by itself. To sustain your recovery, you will still need to attend regular recovery meetings. This is why treatment programs will connect you with Anonymous programs while you are still in treatment.

If all this sounds like a lot of work, it is. If misery addiction were easy to handle, you'd have fixed it yourself by now.

On the other hand, after the first six months to a year, recovery isn't nearly as difficult as addiction. Addiction is painful every single day in terms of anguish, cost, missed opportunities, and messed-up intimacy. Recovery is hard at first, but it gets easier as time goes on. It starts being worth the effort right away.

CAN'T I JUST GO TO THERAPY?

Therapy is good. Therapy is where you can heal from childhood neglect and abuse, experience a safe bond, and learn relationship skills. But unless your misery addiction is quite mild (i.e., you don't fall into the self-sabotaging or miserable categories on the continuum on page 137), therapy alone won't be enough. As Bill W., a founder of AA, wrote in 1939: "Surely this was the answer— self-knowledge. But it was not, for the frightful day came when I drank once more. The curve of my declining moral and bodily health fell off like a ski-jump."[1]

Therapy is powerful, and it goes very well with the recovery process, but it does not replace it. Each is enhanced by the other.

COMPONENTS OF RECOVERY

Community

Few addicts of any stripe recover in isolation. In fact, addiction thrives on isolation. When we are alone too much, we don't have other minds balancing our sometimes extreme thoughts. Plus too much loneliness may send us to our addiction for relief.

To enter and sustain recovery, we must join the other courageous folks who took the chance of doing something different in the face of their own pain. In any recovery community you find these miraculous people, survivors who endured withdrawal and surrendered their self-centeredness on a bet that felt risky at the time—a bet that their own lives could be different.

When you listen to recovering addicts, you often hear phrases such as, "I didn't think I could ever give up gambling," or "I was sure I'd be the one who failed at recovery," or "If it could work for me, as sunk as I was, it would work for anybody." They know how difficult it is. They've been there. And they are your best guides out of the haunted forest.

Hanging out with recovering people gives you an attitude adjustment, reminds you of how the recovery process works, gives you practical tips for handling the details of overhauling an entire life, and creates a lot of laughter.

Abstinence

This is the news that might sound bad at first. To be in recovery, you need to be abstinent from your addiction.

It makes sense. Practicing your addiction is the antithesis of recovery. As long as your eyes are on your addiction, they are not on recovery.

Directing your attention toward recovery puts you in an entirely different mind-set than when you are thinking about how terrible your life is (or how terrible you are), or when to shop or eat addictively, or how to do something to hurt yourself.

Recovery lets you step into an alternate universe. It alters and enhances your consciousness.

Here's some really good news: you don't have to be abstinent in order to go to a recovery meeting. You go to a meeting in order to get and stay abstinent. The only requirement is the desire to stop doing your addiction.

Abstinence for a misery addict gets complicated. An alcoholic stops drinking; a gambler stops gambling; a food addict stops eating trigger foods. What does a misery addict do?

You stop sabotaging yourself. You

- stop doing things that cause you loss or pain and start doing things that create positive results.
- stop doing things that zone you out and start practicing mindfulness.
- stop using tool addictions and start caring for yourself.
- stop avoiding people, situations, and emotions and start feeling.
- stay away from people and places that trigger your addiction and spend time with people who support your recovery.
- avoid people who are mean to you and join with people who care about you in a healthy way.

That's a lot. Yet it can be done. Many others have done it.

Surrender

Admitting to powerlessness is the starting point of recovery. As long as we think we can control our addictions, we are operating out of an illusion.

We have no control over an addiction. The addiction is control-ling us. It's only our own addictive thinking that tells us that we can have control over this thing we can't stay away from.

An addiction makes us try to control and manipulate other people. Directly or indirectly, we try to get them to support our ad-diction. We try to control how people view us, what the guy in the next car is doing, how fast the grass grows.

The addiction influences our minds and our thinking. It tells us we are better than some people and worse than others. It keeps us busy thinking about when we're going to get our next fix—whether it's a drug, a food, a stretch of computer game-playing, or a bout of avoidance, frustration, failure, and self-criticism.

The addiction tells us we don't have an addiction. It's a type of brainwashing, and we are its hostages.

We are not in control, not even of our own minds.

Admitting to this is the starting place.

Once we honor the truth—that we are powerless in the face of the power of the addiction—we make an internal shift that is recep-tive to the other realities of recovery. We understand that we can't find abstinence by ourselves. We realize that we need a strength greater than ours alone to get anywhere.

Surrender is different from either compliance or sacrifice. Com-pliance means just going along with the program, while internally criticizing others and trying to manipulate them. Sacrifice is giving yourself away to someone or something else. In contrast, surrender is about letting go of trying to control what, paradoxically, we never had control of in the first place.

The Basic Program

The blueprint for change in any Anonymous group is called the Twelve Steps. The first of these Steps is an acknowledgment of our personal powerlessness over our addiction.

Once you achieve abstinence, it will become clear that the prob-lem is not just with the addiction: the deeper problem is with liv-ing. Thus the Twelve Steps help us transform our relationships with ourselves and with others.

The Support of a Sponsor

Addicts have trouble asking for and accepting help. "I'd like to do it myself, thank you." Recovery, being the opposite of addiction, gives us increasing practice at using help. Twelve Step groups and programs have a formal system for it called sponsorship.

It can be hard to spontaneously ask a stranger to listen to us when we're having trouble. It becomes somewhat easier if we've made an arrangement with a person we have at least met—someone who is expecting us to call.

A sponsor is anyone who has more experience in the recovery program than you do. She becomes your personal guide into the program, helping you achieve abstinence, supporting you through the rough bumps, and shepherding you up the Steps. She does this in part by helping you create a structure to follow. At first this will probably involve calling her once a day and going to a certain number of meetings a week.

As your relationship and trust grow, you will discover that you can be completely honest about what you are feeling and get helpful direction in response. (I can assure you that there is nothing that you have done or thought that someone else in recovery has not also done or thought.)

How do you get a sponsor? You listen at meetings, and when someone's experience or integrity appeals to you, you simply ask him if he will sponsor you.

You may be thinking, *Why would someone do this for me? It's asking too much.* Or, *I don't want to embarrass someone who might want to turn me down.* Or, *What if she says no? I'll be mortified.*

First, it's not asking too much. In fact, it's asking just the right amount because it's a central part of working your recovery program.

Second, you don't have to worry about embarrassing someone else or putting pressure on him by asking for his help. People with recovery experience know how to take care of themselves. In fact, by being your sponsor, someone *is* taking care of himself. He knows that by helping you with your program, his own recovery will be strengthened.

Third, it's indeed quite possible that the person you ask might say no. She might be going through a very busy period, or she might already be sponsoring all the people she can handle—in which case, it's important to her own recovery that she turns you down. So if someone does say no, you help both yourself and her if you simply ask another. (See how in recovery everyone naturally helps each other?)

If a sponsorship turns out to be a bad fit, it's okay to change sponsors. Sometimes people have both an abstinence sponsor and a Step sponsor.

In Twelve Step programs, it's customary (but not required) for your sponsor to be the same gender as you.

A Higher Power

All Twelve Step programs encourage participants to surrender control—not to some other person, but to what the programs call a Higher Power.

You get to decide what this Higher Power is for you. It can be God, or the Goddess, or Jesus, or Allah. It doesn't have to be religious at all. It can be your recovery group. (After all, its members have collectively demonstrated power over an addiction that had beaten them individually into the ground. If that's not a Higher Power, then I don't know what is.)

No one will ask you who or what your Higher Power is, and you do not have to have this worked out before you go to a meeting.

While Twelve Step programs often meet in churches, they are not affiliated with any particular religion, including the one housing the meeting.

Some recovery programs—which are *not* Twelve Step, Anonymous programs—are affiliated with specific religions or denominations. Some of these are more valuable and effective than others. Your chances for recovery increase if a program includes sponsors and abstinence and if the people in it are comfortable speaking the whole truth.

One problem with many church-run programs is that there can be a denial of the shadow side. If people in the program feel pressured to do well in order to prove their faith in God, they'll have difficulty talking about the things that go wrong. This actually makes abstinence tougher rather than easier. Any program that pressures its participants for success will not be of lasting help. It will only encourage people to try to control the addiction—and in that direction lies failure.

JUST DO IT?

There's a just-do-it school of thought that says, "Just quit smoking. Just stop drinking. Just stop being miserable. There's no need for all this program crap."

It should be very clear by now that, for a misery addict, this is asking too much. The addiction is too subtle and uses too many schemes and devices.

THE TIME OF YOUR LIFE

An addiction squanders time. Recovery gives you your time back for the bargain price of two or three hours a week.

As a client recently said in amazement, "I have so much time! I didn't realize how much time my addiction was taking up."

In recovery, you can discover time to garden, sing, laugh with friends, walk beside the water, watch birds, hold your cat, throw sticks for your dog to chase, cuddle your children, play golf with your partner, and walk steadily toward your deepest dreams. Once you can let yourself receive it, there is no comfort that is as warming or as rejuvenating as the genuine, kind human contact that blossoms with recovery.

CHAPTER TWENTY-ONE

Allergic to Progress—
The Misery Addict's Dilemma

So what happens when the recovery process itself causes aversion for a misery addict?

CONFINED BY STRUCTURE

Aisha's childhood felt like boot camp. Meals were at 7 A.M., noon, and 6 P.M., without fail. If she was late, she got whatever was left over from three hungry brothers, usually the vegetables and fruit. No one would fix her a plate, even if her reason for being late was legitimate, such as a Girl Scout meeting that ran long.

Everyone had chores that had to be accomplished on a certain day and at a certain time. The house was cleaned every Saturday morning. Laundry had to be done by Saturday afternoon. She had to wash the dinner vegetables as soon as she got home from school and finish her homework before supper. Tuesdays and Thursdays, she vacuumed the living room. Wednesdays and Saturdays, she swept the kitchen. On Sundays, her job was to mash the potatoes and wash the dishes. As she got older, she was assigned more responsibility for meals. If she fought any of this, she got switched across the legs.

Parochial school was similar—strict, inflexible class periods; no excuses for late homework; no room for individual interests or variations in ability; humiliating paddling in the halls for infractions.

For her first eighteen years of life, Aisha knew only strict control by others. So when she first got to college, she went wild. She got into drugs. She discovered sex. She got pregnant. Yet she belonged to a generation that insisted on marriage, regardless of the skills and temperament of the birth father or her own compatibility with him.

Just like that, her life was controlled again—by the needs of a baby, by a resentful husband, and by poverty.

Twenty years later, free of both child and spouse, she was solidly addicted to misery, not wanting to be unhappy, but knowing no other way to live. Her tool addictions were food, caretaking, shopping, and television.

Aisha couldn't tolerate structure. She never did anything the same way two days in a row if she could help it. She had to work, but most days she slept until minutes before she had to throw herself together and dash out the door. After work, she might shop or go through a drive-thru, bring her food home, and eat in front of the TV or else make dinner out of the candy counter at the movie theater. She'd feel vaguely guilty for not doing more productive things, for the mess in the apartment, or for putting off laundry or bill paying, but anytime she said something such as "Tomorrow I'll sit down and pay the bills," her stomach knotted up, and she couldn't make herself follow through.

Structure is useful. By structuring my day, I manage my time. I have a light plan to use my free hour to visit the bank, the library, and the photo shop. Because I have a plan, when I leave home, I know what things to take. This gets items where they belong—out of the house and off my mind.

But it's a light plan. If I run into a friend on the street, I can dump the plan so that we can stop for a cup of tea.

Structure can be as simple as a plan for the day or as complex as a way to juggle and organize several long-term projects. Without structure, our lives get messy. It helps to have a specific place to leave the keys, a method for handling junk mail, a table where you put things that need to go with you the next time you leave.

For Aisha, structure was suffocating. Yet her lack of structure made her life chaotic. It kept her feeling guilty as deadlines ran her down and left her behind. She felt pressured by the tasks hanging over her head—and only got in deeper when she escaped the pressure with a tool addiction. But she could not make herself organize her time.

Recovery from misery addiction can offer Aisha a way out. The hitch? It involves structure. Certain practices must occur each day if she is to fully recover.

Aisha has an aversion to the very thing that can save her.

AVERSION TO MEALTIMES

We first met Merril in chapter 11. Merril's mother was an angry abuser, and her father was passive and never intervened. Merril hated anger and told herself she would not display anger. But she unknowingly discharged anger in the form of barbed teasing.

"Merril, you get in here and sit at this table!"

"I have one more math problem, Mama, and then I'll be done with my homework."

"Don't sass me, girl. Get yourself in here and set yourself down."

"I'm not sassing, Mama. The last time I left my homework, Ezra spilt Pepsi all over it and I had to copy the whole thing over."

"Girl. Here. Now. You are so stubborn. I don't fix these meals to have them get cold. Why you have to buck me every turn, I don't know. You are so much trouble. Why can't you be more like your sister? She's in here eating like a little angel. *Merril, you get in here. Now!*"

With that a dam broke, and Merril's mother began screaming obscenities at Merril, stomping into the other room, and dragging her to the kitchen table. Meanwhile, Merril's dad sat quietly and continued eating.

Merril wasn't instantly obedient, but she had a plausible case and she tried to negotiate. In any case, her behavior was not reason enough for her mother to pop her cork.

Many times Merril came to the table on time, and most of the time she did her mealtime chores. Yet her mother still targeted her.

"Merril, you can't have those potatoes. You're fat enough already. Cece, here have some potatoes."

"I didn't make you a birthday cake, Honey, 'cause we both know you've got some weight to lose. Here, blow out the candle on this pineapple."

Not surprisingly, grown-up Merril had an aversion to seated meals and to nutritious food. She craved the foods, starches, and sweets that had been forbidden her as a child. For Merril, food, especially food eaten at a table with others, symbolized exposure and humiliation.

Just sitting at a dinner table with friends aroused such fury and rebellion in her that she would revert to her usual method of expressing anger—barbed teasing. Some friends didn't know what to do with it. Some tried to engage in playful banter but then got stung when it intensified. Some tried to set boundaries, which to Merril felt like the arbitrary, punitive rules imposed by her mother. A boundary-setter would become, in Merril's mind, someone to defeat, either through passive resistance or more subtle teasing.

Of course, this damaged her relationships. Despite her loving nature at other times, people would distance from her and not even be able to articulate just what it was that caused them to back off.

Merril considered missing meals an emblem of honor and would use such information to create issues with people who cared about her.

"Honey, sit down," said Merril's husband. "Join us for dinner."

"No. I had some salad while I was fixing dinner."

"Have you eaten today?" he said.

"No. I didn't feel like it."

And then a tug-of-war would ensue, which Merril would win through defiance.

Here's a bases-loaded situation. Merril, like any human, needs regular meals each day. Yet mealtimes for Merril triggered rage and fear.

We humans have a propensity for coming together over meals. It's a tribal need, ancient in our instincts, and it could offer Merril a feeling of belonging. But since, for Merril, social meals were fraught with humiliation, she didn't eat with others if at all possible. She ate alone, unobserved, usually after fasting for most of the day.

Her erratic eating caused her to have uneven energy, bouts of tiredness, and lackluster involvement in life. When she couldn't escape a meal with others, her barbed anger cost her intimacy and turned away people who would otherwise have offered her support.

To recover from her misery addiction, Merril needs to nourish herself with regular, healthy meals in order to have the energy and clarity of thought that recovery requires. She will eventually have to express the anger that, for her, is connected to mealtimes so that meals lose their triggering power.

However, the very aspects required for progress—regular meals, healthy foods, relaxed social meals, and healthy expression of anger—are aversive to Merril.

I've found hundreds of examples of this kind of cross-wiring among misery addicts. Childhood trauma or abuse creates a negative association with something that promotes well-being or success. Unable to force themselves to embrace the positive action, they end up losing out on something that makes life work.

With repetition the destructive action becomes more and more familiar, and that which is familiar feels safe. It may not really *be* safe, but to our individual perspective, it *feels* safe. Over time, then, we gain a positive emotional bond to a negative, self-destructive deed.

At the same time, the opposite, healthy action, which is needed to promote recovery, has become symbolic of age-old repression or abuse. Thus the ingredients for recovery in themselves can trigger anxiety and distress.

This is the central reason why recovery from a misery addiction is so difficult—and why accepting help from others and turning to a recovery program are usually essential.

CAPSIZING SUPPORT

"Akilah, I know you asked me to not call at the last minute, but I just realized my winter gown has a spot on it, and the Christmas party is tonight."

Akilah was silent.

Tonya persisted. "Please, Akilah, it's an emergency. I'm up for a promotion, and I need this to go right."

Akilah sighed. "Okay, Tonya, but get it here in fifteen minutes or I'm out of here. Christmas is a holiday for me too, you know, and I have things to get done myself."

"Thank you, Akilah. I know. I'll make it up to you."

Right, Akilah said to herself, looking around at the racks of dry cleaning ready for pickup. *Like you did all the other times you had an emergency.*

Tonya is about to lose a friend by not taking responsibility for her part of a transaction. The phrase "I know you asked me to not, but . . ." always spells problems for a friendship. It translates to "I'm about to violate a boundary you set because my need is more important than your boundary." A friend's boundary should be violated only in dire emergency—and then only after giving her a real chance to say no. Instead Tonya kept up the pressure, not indicating through her words or attitude that she was receptive to a "no."

Such an attitude sets up resistance in the other person, and eventually something will give. Akilah will lose her generosity toward Tonya, or she'll stop doing things that nurture their friendship, or she'll carry a resentment that will surface in some other situation, like ripping off the dry cleaning tags and letting Tonya's favorite sweater get stuck in the no-tag bin.

Akilah could have said no anyway—and it would have been better all around if she had. It was Tonya's responsibility to take the dress out of her closet early and check its condition days ago, not on the afternoon of the party. It didn't help that then she was at the store in thirty minutes instead of the promised fifteen, and Akilah seethed that again her time and needs were not respected.

Tonya is a charismatic woman who attracts people who want to be generous to her. Yet she disregards their gifts or offerings in a way that causes them to pull back. Because of her lack of planning, she is often in some sort of crisis where she needs a friend's help. But in her distress, she disregards the friend's situation in a way that sets up resentment and creates an unwillingness to help her. Thus Tonya is, subtly and almost continuously, undermining and isolating herself.

We very much need the help of others in order to recover.

Addiction is synonymous with profound isolation. Recovery comes about as a result of the opposite—growing intimacy with a genuinely caring community. Yet most misery addicts, usually unwittingly, create barren isolation for themselves.

Most recovering people are generous. But they also get increasingly better at setting boundaries. When someone gets identified as a perpetual taker who isn't showing an investment in his own recovery, a skilled sponsor might set a final boundary: "I can't sponsor you anymore. Please don't call again."

In this way a misery addict may narrow her field of potential guides through recovery. For a misery addict, alienating sponsors can be like throwing life rafts off the deck of the *Titanic.*

As one of my friends enjoys saying, a lack of planning on your part does not constitute an emergency on my part. In other words, you take your own consequences and learn your own lesson.

HAZARDOUS SUPPORT

"Fabia, make the potato salad for the church picnic."

"I don't know how, Mama."

"Of course you do. I've made potato salad hundreds of times right in front of you."

"I didn't realize I was going to have to make it."

"Do you think it's okay to sit on your fat behind and not help?"

"No, Mama. I'll help. Tell me how. Please help me."

"Do I have to do everything around here? Do you want me to tell your father that you won't do a simple thing like make potato salad? Should I have you stand up at the church picnic while I tell everyone you're too stupid to make potato salad? Figure it out. And don't leave a mess.

"Oh, and you know what else? You ruined your new Sunday dress. You're not going to get another one, so you'll have to wear your school clothes on Sunday."

"Mama, no one wears their school uniform to church. I'll be embarrassed."

"You should have thought of that before you ruined your dress."

"How did I ruin it?"

"You washed it."

"You told me to wash my dirty clothes."

"But you don't wash Dacron unless it says you can. Otherwise it shrinks and puckers like your dress did."

"I didn't know that."

"Well, stupid, that's what the label's for."

"What do you mean?"

"The label in the back of the neck—it tells you how to clean your outfit."

"I didn't know that, Mama."

"Well, you do now."

Fabia had no shot at intimacy in her household. Her mother's constant smoldering anger prevented her from realizing that Fabia needed to be taught life skills and gave her zero tolerance for Fabia's mistakes, which Fabia was bound to make because she had no guidance. Whenever Fabia asked how to do something, her mother ridiculed her for her stupidity. If she asked a simple question such as "How come tulips don't bloom again?" she was castigated so harshly she'd collapse inside.

Fabia's father was so completely engrossed in his work, doling out punishment on command from his wife, that Fabia couldn't draw close to him either. Fabia had no one to turn to for arbitration or coziness for her first seventeen years. She associated family with injustice and closeness with punishment, so as an adult, she expected friends to be arbitrary and angry with her for no predictable reason.

Thus she was tentative around other people and could not ask for help, no matter how innocuous the problem. She would wander for two hours looking for a doctor's office rather than ask directions and once in that office be unable to ask the questions that would give her relief from needless worry. If her doctor ordered a medical test, she couldn't ask what it would be like or why he thought she should have it.

We might be thinking, *But a doctor is supposed to help. Go ahead and ask. It's his job.*

Helping was her mother's job too. That kind of argument would give Fabia no protection.

To recover we need to accept help. Sooner or later we also need to *ask* for help. Next to abstinence, the single most important facet of recovery is getting and using the support of others.

But for many misery addicts, intimacy is associated with abuse, and asking for help is associated with humiliation.

Remember the information about needing a safe harbor and a secure base in order to venture out into the world? That safe harbor is what we run back to when we get scared. But if the safe harbor is also a source of threat, then we have nowhere to turn for help.

Few addicts can put themselves on the expansive road of recovery on their own. For a misery addict, it's even more of a stretch, because his addiction typically employs other addictions, all of which further increase his isolation.

This is one of the most painful paradoxes of recovery from misery addiction. The misery addict absolutely must use support to make it. Yet all his instincts warn him against revealing himself to others. His life is a study in not getting too close to people. He will do anything rather than ask for help.

He carries a deep aversion to the very thing that would allow him to progress.

BROKEN TREATIES

Ingrid's runner-up addiction, after misery addiction, was co-dependence. After the intensity of weeks of misery addiction treatment, in which Ingrid experienced tremendous breakthroughs, she began sabotaging her program by giving too much of herself. Instead of taking advantage of her prepaid room at her therapist's retreat house, she left it for a few days each week in order to do design work for nice people she didn't want to be with, in a business venture she didn't have a personal interest in and for which she might never be paid.

This is the theme song of misery addiction: leave the place that is helping you to do something you don't enjoy for nice but distant acquaintances for little or no compensation.

A couple of months later, those of us who cared deeply about

Ingrid were distressed to hear that she had been in a potentially fatal car accident. (Fortunately, she survived.) She'd gotten in a car with a slightly drunk driver to travel across town on a busy interstate at night when she had a perfectly good bus pass in her purse and could have been home in fifteen minutes. She'd gotten in the car, not because she wanted to go where the driver was going, but so the driver would have company.

We all know that alcohol, food, and drug addiction can kill. This is one of the ways misery addiction kills.

As Ingrid and I talked about her accident, I asked her where her warning voice had been—the still, small voice that tells us, "This isn't safe. Take care of yourself. Get away, or do this differently."

She said, "It didn't speak."

Why didn't Ingrid's intuition speak that night? She had just successfully completed her misery addiction recovery program. She had done some work on the Twelve Steps. She was still meeting with her groups. What was missing?

This: she was not in abstinence from her addiction to sacrificing herself for other people, and she was not invested in herself.

An obscure theme played by misery addicts is this lack of commitment to themselves, a lack of investment in their own lives.

One of the really difficult lessons a recovering addict has to learn early is to put recovery first. The clamor of other people has to take second place. This goes against the instincts of a misery addict, who sacrifices herself as automatically as a Dalmatian jumps into the fire truck when the fire bell rings.

Part of this self-sacrifice may be noble, but it is also a long-standing defense used as protection against being hurt or abandoned. No matter how it got there, it has to stop.

For a misery addict in early recovery, putting herself first feels selfish. She is afraid of being judged as such by others. She isn't used to having a commitment to herself.

These attitudes work against sustaining a commitment to recovery. And recovery requires a commitment—not just to the process, but to yourself. For the sake of your quality of life, you have to soldier on with recovery through withdrawal and the unfamiliar landscape of a revamped approach to living.

After the first year, things get better faster and faster, and after five years of recovery, you will be really cooking—but the first year takes a lot of work.

You have to be committed to yourself and to the possibility of promise in your life to do that work.

FORGETTING THE PATTERN

Fabia completed five penetrating years of therapeutic work. Within that time, she went to the bottom of her inner self where she had stored the little girl who kept getting set up by an angry mother who used her husband like a sword of vengeance.

Her inner child had stored many of her memories and most of her pain, so opening to this part of herself was no picnic for Fabia. This little girl was terrified.

Therapy does more than clean our basements. It's an opportunity to discover our personal patterns. By seeing these patterns we unearth the forgotten cruelties that shaped our lives.

Getting conscious about patterns enables us to predict ourselves. We can learn our likely reaction to a future situation and prepare when we're heading into personal swampland. We can even learn to avoid certain swamps altogether.

In the depths of therapy, Fabia learned the patterns exhibited by her own little inner self when she got scared. Then after much courageous work, Fabia got married. She decided to cut back on therapy because she was so happy and wanted to put all of her focus on her marriage.

Fabia made a great choice in men. Her new husband was gentle, attentive, and good at communicating. He adored her.

However, being in a marriage recalled for Fabia the essence of family life. Her only experience of family life had been harsh and punitive, and she couldn't stop herself from responding to her husband as if he would hurt her.

She'd go to the grocery and get paralyzed that she was picking the wrong type of oranges or that he'd be furious with her if she got chicken instead of pork. She'd take too long; she'd either buy every kind or none at all, and then approach him so timidly afterward that he'd feel irritated with her. He couldn't get her to see him as himself, and her way of cowering made him feel like an ogre.

What do you think was going on here?

Fabia forgot her pattern. She entered a situation that triggered past experiences and didn't remember that a part of her psyche needed special protection as soon as she felt threatened.

Her pattern was swallowing her, and since a part of her old pattern was to not ask for help, as that pattern got more activated, she became less able to ask for help or call for a therapy appointment. Over time, with decreasing support and increasing threat, she was in danger of jeopardizing her opportunity for intimacy and even her marriage.

Self-care would have looked like this: Fabia enters her marriage, feels afraid, and isn't able to tell her husband that she is scared of displeasing him. She has two red flags: a feeling and a behavior. The feeling is fear and the behavior is an inability to say something important. Either flag is a good enough reason to go back into therapy or to turn to her support group.

The next step is to talk long enough at a therapy session or recovery meeting to identify what's wrong and to experience the shift that lets her return to adult consciousness.

Fabia did the opposite. She kept walking deeper into her old pattern without getting help, which caused her to operate from an ever-younger level of her internal self.

What kind of person goes deeper into an emotional landscape that unsettles her? A person who has been trained to stop thinking. A person who has been punished for not going forward, even though going forward becomes increasingly hurtful.

Fabia was constantly set up by her mother to go forward into a task she did not know how to do and then ridiculed or deprived when she did it wrong. It made her afraid to risk, yet it also taught her to keep going no matter what.

Misery addicts survive traumatic childhoods by training themselves to go against their natural instincts. This causes them to misplace their own internal road maps.

Baby humans have the capacity to construct an internal working model of the environment and of their own actions with it.[1] The more adequate that model, the more accurately a child can predict the future. If something in the environment becomes drastically unpredictable, a preverbal infant signals his response with gestures and emotions. As he becomes more verbal, he attempts to use language to understand the change. By discussing it, he can add extensions to his model of how the world works.

Parents who cut off discussion about departures from the expected abort a child's attempt to revise her road map. ("Never mind why your father canceled the picnic. We aren't going to discuss it.") A household filled with chaos teaches a child that the world is chaotic. What good is a map? This can lead to an adult who has thrown out her road map or has lost her map-reading skills.

Fabia's home was at the mercy of her mother's anger. That *was* the pattern but one far too subtle for a child who was told that everything was her fault.

It was impossible for Fabia to predict the future based on her own instincts, so as an adult, she overruled her instincts whenever she was in a threatening situation. Of course, that's when she needed her instincts the most.

She was then unable to use the thing that would protect her— her knowledge of her own process.

This is common among misery addicts. What can be so obvious to a friend or a therapist is invisible to her. We perceive her as setting herself up when what she is doing is falling back into a pattern about which and within which she's unconscious.

AVERSION TO THE TOOLS OF RECOVERY

The central dilemma for a misery addict is this: the tools he employed for survival as a child now cripple him as an adult. Meanwhile, the tools that make recovery work seem threatening, frightening, or pointless. The misery addict has to let go of his old, comfortable, familiar tools and start using new ones. And the new ones feel just like what hurt him when he was young.

For the misery addict, any of these can taste like ashes: structure, support, good self-care, help, mindfulness, a commitment to

oneself, groups, trusting others, being known, experiencing feelings, putting oneself first, and using intuition. Recovery itself feels
threatening.

This is why a misery addict may often need to start with therapy. The goal of this therapy is to create a secure bond with the
therapist so that she becomes the addict's secure base and safe
haven. From that shelter, the addict can then venture forth into the
adventure of recovery, touching base frequently and routinely with
the therapist to work through the dilemmas posed by the recovery
process.

CHAPTER TWENTY-TWO

Step One

Step One. *We admitted we were powerless over self-sabotage—that our lives had become unmanageable.*

Powerless? You bet. There's no way you can just buck up, throw your shoulders back, and fix your misery addiction on your own—not if it's a genuine misery addiction instead of a mild leaning.

Recovery involves community. Your first community was frightful.

Recovery involves consciousness. Consciousness brings you contact with pain and fear.

Recovery involves structure. When you were a wee one, structure may have enslaved you.

Recovery requires commitment. You likely gave up on your commitment to yourself and your future some time back.

This is powerlessness served on a platter.

What can you do with so much against you?

Surrender. Stop fighting.

Your recovery from an addiction to misery starts here, now.

The *Twelve Steps and Twelve Traditions* of Alcoholics Anonymous talks about the difficulty of admitting complete defeat.[1] Now let's apply that problem to misery addiction.

Who wants to admit to defeat? Not me. It is truly painful to admit that, through inaction or indecision or a tool addiction (for example, to eating, working, or game-playing), we have distorted our thinking into such enormous avoidance and resistance that only an act of God can release us from practicing our misery addiction.

No other kind of defeat is like this. Avoidance and misery, now our stalkers, bleed us of our self-sufficiency and our will to resist their demands.

Let's look at how Overeaters Anonymous talks about it.

In OA we learn that a lack of willpower isn't what makes us compulsive eaters. In fact, compulsive overeaters often exhibit an exceptional amount of willpower. But compulsive eating is an illness that cannot be controlled by willpower. None of us decided to have this disorder, any more than we would have decided to have any other disease. We can now cease blaming ourselves or others for our compulsive eating.

. . . Whatever the cause, today we are not like normal people when it comes to eating. . . . We can't quit. A normal eater gets full and loses interest in food. We compulsive overeaters crave more.[2]

Let's translate this for misery addiction:

We've learned that a lack of willpower is not what makes us misery addicts. In fact, misery addicts often exhibit an exceptional amount of willpower. We can be quite stubborn when someone tries to help us and positively mulelike if someone tries to move us forward when we don't want to go. But misery addiction is an illness that can't be controlled by willpower. We didn't choose to have this disorder any more than we would have decided to have any other disease. Therefore, we can stop blaming ourselves and others for our compulsion to sabotage ourselves.

Whatever the cause, today we are not like normal people when it comes to being kind to ourselves. We can't do it. A normal person, if he hurts himself, stops doing the thing that hurts. We are different. When we are hurtful to ourselves, we can't quit. We go on sabotaging ourselves and hesitate when positive action is needed.

We've been beating ourselves up for years. Yet that hasn't worked. No matter how severely we castigate ourselves, no matter how much shame we heap upon our heads, it does not inspire us to move. No amount of self-blame has gotten us anywhere.

Whenever we've tried to force ourselves out of inertia or tool addictions, it hasn't lasted. Sooner or later we rebelled against the structures set up for us (by ourselves or by other people) no matter what it cost.

We've made autonomy a god. We will fight for our independence to the last inch, even if it drowns us. We would rather be defeated by our own decision, or even by our indecision, than succeed by another's plan.

We seek revenge for past wrongs by taking our anger out on people who care about us. We fail to plan and then expect others to rescue us. We ask too much or too little of the people who try to help us. We give too much of ourselves to others, sacrificing something personally important, and then we resent it. We set ourselves up and then blame others.

We've lost friends, jobs, money, and, most of all, time. We've lost months and years of our life to rebellion and inertia.

We are angry, but we hide it and turn it against ourselves.

When we see that our impulses have carried us too far, we try to exert control over ourselves. When we see that we've been swept into the nets of a tool addiction, we try to control ourselves out of the addiction. But control doesn't work.

We need to say this again. *Control doesn't work.*

If we continue to try to control something that can't be controlled, we keep ourselves stuck in our addiction to misery. Trying to do something in a way that can't work is our specialty. We are notorious for trying again and again with methods that are sure to fail.

Control *can't* work. Millions of addicts have proven this—to themselves and others—countless times. If you look at your own life, you'll see that you've already proven it to yourself.

Now is the time to let this struggle go.

All you have to do is admit defeat. Then, and only then, grace can enter. Admitting defeat isn't that bad. It's just the simple truth. You've been defeated by avoidance, rebellion, misery, and addiction, and each one is bigger than you are.

All you have to do is give up what hasn't been working.

Simply surrender to the truth—that you are powerless over the yearning to avoid pain, loneliness, and anger. You are powerless over your resistance to being controlled by others. You are powerless over the people who have hurt you in the past. You are powerless over self-sabotage. You are powerless over your unkindness to yourself. Your life has been unmanageable, and no efforts on your part to straighten it out have worked because the addiction kept overriding your best intentions.

Here is what the tens of millions of people in recovery from addictions will tell you: When you surrender to the truth, the door to grace will burst open. And soon afterward you will be able to say the following:

We admitted we were powerless, and then everything changed. We admitted we were powerless, and then the hardness dropped from our hearts. We became open to the wisdom of others. We became able to laugh at our own stubbornness. We actually laughed at our foibles and felt the balm that comes from realizing we were not alone after all.

We admitted we were powerless, and we relaxed into the company of good people who spoke deep truths, who had seen the light of deliverance, and who knew ways to walk toward it.

We had been afraid of falling into negative thinking, but admitting to powerlessness turned out to be a simple truth. As with all truths, it opened a door. After living a life torn with paradox, we embraced this paradox: admitting powerlessness allowed spiritual power to flow.

We had to admit it. We didn't just simply state it. We had to drag it out of ourselves the first few times. We admitted it only after seeing that our false pride was getting us nowhere. Even in the company of those who'd gone before us, we felt shamefaced to say we were addicted.

But then a strange thing happened. We said it, and people smiled at us and welcomed us by name. We were accepted in our condition, not shunned.

Everything changed. Then we could relax. We could lay down our weapons. We were safe in the company of those who had traveled the road ahead of us. We could know peace.

CHAPTER TWENTY-THREE

The Next Steps

Step Two. *Came to believe that a Power greater than ourselves could restore us to sanity.*

In Overeaters Anonymous's version of the Twelve Step classic *Twelve Steps and Twelve Traditions,* we read, "'Restore me to sanity? I don't need that. I'm perfectly sane. I just have an eating problem.' But how sane are we, really?"[1]

It's a good question. How sane are we when we deprive ourselves of breakfast, knowing that we'll pay later by eating too much at lunch and losing energy in the afternoon? How sane is it to spend three hours playing games on the computer when we're already tired from a day of work? How sane is it to stop taking a medication that has been helping? How sane is it to put off a recovery experience that could lift us out of our self-defeating ways?

Insanity is doing the same thing and expecting different results. We go shopping when our credit card is maxed out and we already have enough clothes to last us till the next millennium. We turn to a tool addiction to feel better, knowing in the long run we'll only feel worse about ourselves and have lost yet more time and money.

So maybe we do need to be restored to sanity.

Came to believe that a Power greater than ourselves could restore us to sanity. For some misery addicts this is the hardest part. People who feel betrayed by God don't have much interest in trusting God again. People who were harmed and twisted up by religion don't want anything more to do with it.

That's fine. Misery Addicts Anonymous—MAA—is not a religion. You don't have to believe in God or even in religion. You just have to pick some Power greater than yourself.

Here is what people in recovery will tell you:

We didn't have to believe from the start. We just had to be open to the possibility of believing. We had to give ourselves room for belief to grow. By being open we could let in the evidence of the people sitting right in front of us. They had surrendered, and then they let themselves believe that something greater than themselves could do the impossible. And it worked!

They got separated from their addictions, and their lives turned around, and they were sitting right there, happy about it. Some even stated they were grateful to their addiction because without it they wouldn't have found this great way of living that had led to such riches in friendship, joy, and serenity.

We didn't have to actually believe in this Power. We just had to make room in our minds for the possibility that a Power greater than ourselves was powerful.

What's so hard about that?

As writer Joe McQ says in his wonderful book *The Steps We Took,* "Believing is the state of mind we must have before beginning any project. . . . Belief is an awesome force."[2] McQ points out that believing sets limits. If someone believes she can't get a better job, then she can't. On the other hand, someone believed we could reach the moon, and we did. Further expanding on the concept of a Higher Power, the Hazelden text *A Program for You* says the following:

> That there is a Power greater than our *self*—our individual ego—is as much a fact as our physical existence. This Higher Power has been here all our lives, and throughout the lives of everyone who has ever lived on this planet. It's nothing new. We can call it our conscience, our inner intelligence, the Spirit, the Supreme Being, or God. What we call it isn't important. . . . Most of us have experienced this Power from

time to time—as an inspiration, a presence, or an intelligence. Often, it takes the form of a voice somewhere within us, usually deep down. . . . Now if it's true that God dwells within each human being, that means that each of us has his or her own personal God or Higher Power. And each of us and our own Higher Power can come together in simple and understandable terms. You don't have to worry about whether the God of your understanding is the God of the Baptists or the Catholics or the Jews or the Hindus. You don't necessarily need a priest, a complex philosophy, or someone else's sanction to have a Higher Power. You don't even have to call your Higher Power "God."[3]

First we surrendered. Then making room in our hearts for belief in restoration from a greater power created an impetus that began moving forward under its own steam as long as we kept ourselves connected with the recovery community. Renewed connection with recovery meetings provided the fertile soil for belief to grow.

Week after week we heard surrender and belief applied to every problem under the sun and then working every single time. It's not just that someone without a job got a job or someone who had no place to live found a home. It's that while jobless or homeless and maybe even scared, they were still trusting, still surrendering, still taking essential steps while releasing the outcome. It's so inspiring we found ourselves believing without even working at it. There was too much evidence proving the process works.

Step Three. *Made a decision to turn our will and our lives over to the care of God as we understood God.*

We just make a decision. That's it. Make a decision and our Higher Power (which, again, doesn't have to be anyone else's idea of God) takes it from there.

Step Three is about willingness: our willingness to let go of control and give our Higher Power a shot. We can always take it back if we don't like the results.

In fact, sometimes we *will* take it back even when we like the results. That's why we have to stay in touch with recovering people on a regular basis. Left to ourselves, the old thinking will creep in, and we'll start doing things that cause our recovery to deteriorate.

The decision we made was to turn over our will and our lives, not just the addiction. Why does it have to be so comprehensive?

Because, once we are addicted to something, the addiction takes over our entire lives. If we say we want to quit smoking, the addiction doesn't care. It doesn't pull back and go on its way. It calls us back to the tobacco twenty-seven minutes later on its usual schedule.

Twelve Steps and Twelve Traditions reminds us that the more we depend upon a Higher Power, the more independent we actually become.[4]

The Overeaters Anonymous version of *Twelve Steps and Twelve Traditions* puts it this way:

> It is impossible to take step three until we have taken the first two steps. Once we have fully acknowledged our fatal powerlessness and have come to believe that there is a solution, however, the third step is simple. If we want to live free of the killing disease of compulsive eating, we accept help without reservation from a Power greater than ourselves. We now say yes to this Power, deciding from here on to follow spiritual guidance in making every decision.
>
> Note that we have said this step is simple; we have not said it is easy. It is not easy, because for every one of us this decision means we must now adopt a new and unfamiliar way of thinking and acting on life.[5]

In *A Woman's Way through the Twelve Steps,* author Stephanie Covington adds, "Step Three tells us we can let go of our burden. . . . We can't grow in our recovery if we keep trying to change things beyond our power to change. We get weighed down trying to do the impossible. This distracts us from attending to what we really can change."[6]

What a relief to stop trying what can't work! What a relief to be able to let go. We let ourselves sink into the benevolence of our recovery community, and we start listening.

OTHER STEPS

Nine more Steps follow the three previous ones. When you go to a recovery meeting, you'll learn what they are. These first three have to be worked before proceeding to the rest. And while you might work most of the others for certain periods of time and then move on, these first Steps must be returned to routinely.

CHAPTER TWENTY-FOUR

Recovery Meetings

Is a Twelve Step program the only effective type of recovery program for a misery addict?

No. Other types of programs offer paths out of addiction. If one of those appeals to you, go ahead and try it. But if that program totters, don't throw in the towel. Remember to come back to the granddaddy of the recovery process—any program that ends in the words *anonymous* or *anon* (as in Alcoholics Anonymous or Al-Anon).

It is typical of misery addicts, and any kind of addict, to say, "Oh, I have a better plan over here. Why should I waste my time with a program that has liberated tens of millions of people when by taking this remedy for $29.95, I can change my attitude in a month?"

Go ahead and try your sidetrack. Just remember you have a great option to come back to.

Misery Addicts Anonymous (MAA) is new. As I write this, the center of MAA is in the Pacific Northwest. Someday, I hope, there will be MAA groups all over the world. (If you want to start one in your area, write or e-mail MAA at the addresses on page 271.)

Until you have an MAA meeting near you, however, you can find any open Twelve Step meeting and try it out.

How do you find meetings? Your library may have meetings posted on its bulletin board. Your newspaper may have meetings listed in its community events calendar. Go to the Web sites listed in appendix C of this book, or look in the phone book under AA

and Alcoholics Anonymous (the most widespread of the Anonymous groups) and/or under the names of any of the other Twelve
Step groups. Call and they'll know of open meetings near you.
They'll give you a contact number for each meeting. Call that number to make sure

- it still meets.
- it still meets at the time and place listed.
- it is still an open meeting. (A small percentage of Twelve
  Step meetings are not open to newcomers.)

You may have to shop around to find a meeting that fits you.
Remember that you, like most addicts, can be very particular about
things that don't matter in the larger scheme. The fact that people
wear too much green is not a good reason to reject a meeting.

If you go in with a big chip on your shoulder, you will find
something wrong with it. If you need to prove this can't work for
you, you'll have no trouble finding a reason to not go back. So I
dare you. Attend meetings biweekly for one month before quitting.

WORKING THE PROGRAM

To really work the program, here are my suggestions for getting
started:

For at least the first three to four months, go to at least three
meetings a week.

By the second week, begin talking.

Before the end of the second week, find someone at one of the
meetings whom you respect and appreciate and ask if this person
will sponsor you. If the person says no, ask other group members
whom you genuinely respect until you find a willing sponsor.

To get the most out of your relationship with your sponsor, use
the guidelines on the next page. (Feel free to photocopy the guidelines and give them to a sponsor from another Anonymous program
so he can know how to best assist with your recovery from misery
addiction. The sponsor might also benefit from reading appendix
A.) Most people do better choosing a sponsor of the same gender.

Calling Your Sponsor

Call your sponsor each day and follow these guidelines:

You: Hi. Here's my recovery call.

Sponsor: Good.

Y: I'm powerless over self-sabotage, but my Higher Power can help, so I'm turning my day over to Him/Her and calling you is part of that.

S: Well done. What part of your day is most vulnerable to self-sabotage?

Y: (Answer)

S: How can you set it up for success?

Y: (Answer)

S: On a scale of one to ten, how willing are you to carry out your plan?

Y: (Answer)

S: (If five or less) What's going on? What happened that could be causing you to avoid or resist? Go back to when your attitude changed, and talk about what happened.

S: (If six to eight) What would help you be more willing? Do you need to talk about something, an anxiety or fear?

S: (If nine or ten) Terrific!

S: Did you use a tool addiction since the last time we talked?

Y: (Honest answer)

S: (If yes) You need a meeting. Which one will you go to?

S: (If no) Very well done. What meeting are you going to next?

Y: (Commit to a meeting.)

S: Good. And you'll call again at our usual time tomorrow?

Y: (Commit to next call.)

S: Remember, SSS! Set up for Success; then Surrender.

Y and S: Bye.

Start each day by saying the first three Steps out loud. (See the Twelve Steps for the misery addict on pages 262.)

TWELVE STEP MEETING ETIQUETTE

If you've never been to a Twelve Step meeting before, here's what to expect—and what to do.

First, arrive on time. Twelve Step meetings start promptly.

When someone asks if there are any newcomers, say aloud, "I'm (your first name), and I'm not an alcoholic (overeater, compulsive gambler, etc.), but I think I could be addicted to misery." Pause here; everyone will say hi and your name. Then add, "I hope you'll let me come to this meeting because there aren't any MAA meetings yet in this area, and I'm thinking about working a recovery program to see if it'll help."

Throughout the meeting, listen quietly. When someone talks, everyone else will listen respectfully, but there is no feedback at the end of someone's talk. If someone says something that you want to respond to, *don't*. There is no cross-talk in a recovery meeting. This means if you have an idea that might help someone who talks about a problem, you don't offer it. If you have an opinion about somebody's comments, you don't say it. After the meeting, you can go up to that person and offer it—but remember, you're there to focus on your own recovery, not that of others.

If you feel like saying something, take a turn. You can say anything you want about yourself. But talk about yourself. Don't comment on the talks of others. You might hear others making reference to what someone else said, and that's okay, but as a newcomer, stay away from that until you see how it's done.

Plus, remember that you are here for your addiction, and focusing on others is probably a part of it. You are to focus on yourself, so do that.

Never repeat the stories of others that you hear in meetings to anyone outside of the meetings—even the people you're closest to. Don't talk about whom you saw at a meeting. And if you run into someone whom you know from a meeting outside of that meeting, continue to protect her anonymity. (For example, don't say in front of others, "Oh, I know Julia from a Twelve Step meeting I go to.") Everyone's safety depends on everyone respecting the tradition of anonymity. (See appendix A for additional information.)

One problem with many AA meetings is that they often have sugary things sitting somewhere. If an aspect of your addiction is using food to zone out, stay away from that food, particularly at a meeting. You will set yourself up for trouble if you start to associate eating with recovery meetings. If necessary, find another meeting.

Some aspects of your misery addiction are identical to alcoholism and other forms of addiction. Some are unique to a misery addiction. Some are unique to you.

In the following chapters you'll learn how to tailor your own recovery.

CHAPTER TWENTY-FIVE

Abstinence

The wise authors of *A Program for You* tell us, "The very first thing you have to do to solve a problem is find out what that problem is. This sounds simple, but it often isn't. In order to find a real, lasting solution, you have to understand the problem thoroughly and know exactly what it is. Until you have this information, you can't solve your problem. If your roof is leaking, you can't begin to fix it until you find the hole."[1]

Abstinence is more complex for recovering misery addicts than it is for most other people. Recovering alcoholics stay abstinent from booze, food addicts from trigger foods, drug addicts from drugs, and so on. But since misery addiction often uses a group of addictions to do its dirty work, abstinence revolves on two pivots: ceasing self-sabotage *and* eliminating the use of these tool addictions—addictions used in service of creating avoidance, confusion, resistance, unhappiness, self-criticism, and so on.

It's too difficult to quit everything at once unless you are willing to give yourself the enormous gift of treatment, where you can be protected from both self-sabotage and any and all tool addictions—and be well taken care of at the same time.

If this isn't possible, then you'll need to sort through your list of tool addictions and narrow your initial abstinence to something manageable.

Your complete honesty is necessary for the rest of your program to work. You will have to admit to yourself any addictions and compulsive behaviors you use to soothe your emotions, protect yourself, or check out from reality.

One excellent place to start is by filling out the Substance Inventory chart. Simply put an X in the appropriate column for any substance or behavior you use to avoid feeling pain or to change your mood. For each substance or behavior you use, indicate either "Use daily" or "Use 2 or 3 times a week" and then mark any of the other appropriate boxes.

Substance Inventory

Substance or Behavior	Use daily	Use 2 or 3 times a week	Use to alter con- sciousness	Use to excess	Crave
Alcohol					
Controlled substances (e.g., pot, cocaine)					
Prescription pain medicine					
Narcotics					
Diet pills					
Starches					
Sugary foods					
Fried foods					
Sodas or colas		■			
Nicotine					
Caffeine		■			
Not eating					

If you have checked two or more columns for any substance or behavior, here's a warning: continued use of that substance could interfere with your recovery from misery addiction. Boxes are blackened when that type of usage is not problematic for that substance.

ALCOHOL AND OTHER DRUGS

If you checked at least two columns for alcohol, narcotics, prescription pain medicine (especially if you've healed from the condition that required it), diet pills, or controlled substances such as crack, crank, coke, designer drugs, or pot, then your starting place for recovery is with these addictions. Work a Twelve Step program of recovery for a year; then come back to this book. Complete abstinence from these substances for at least one full year is a prerequisite for your recovery from your misery addiction. (The exception can be prescription pain medicine if you are still suffering from the condition that required it.)

CAFFEINE AND NICOTINE

You can work a recovery program for misery addiction even if you continue smoking and drinking coffee or caffeinated sodas—but if you drink more than five cups a day or chain-smoke, your brain chemistry may interfere with the concentration you'll need.

If you are smoking or caffeinating yourself to that extent, spend at least two weeks reducing or eliminating your nicotine and/or caffeine intake before beginning your recovery from misery addiction. Limit caffeinated beverages to a total of four cups (one quart) a day.

You can try reducing your smoking to two cigarettes an hour. Also try switching to a brand that is lower in nicotine. For many people, however, quitting is easier than tapering off. If this is true in your case, contact your doctor or HMO about a smoking cessation program.

FOOD ADDICTION

Food addictions get seriously in the way of recovery from a misery addiction. Because food is so accessible, it is a quick tool for messing up clarity and providing instant avoidance. Food addiction recovery has to be worked alongside misery addiction recovery. I strongly recommend attending an Overeaters Anonymous group.

Abstinence consists first of not eating any foods that contain refined sugars or NutraSweet (aspartame).

When you achieve abstinence, you will be on your way to remarkable changes in your life. Your preoccupation with food will decrease. Food cravings will weaken and eventually disappear. For the first time, you will be able to make choices about eating.

The room left by departing food obsessions helps you pay better attention to the way you are conducting your life.

ANOREXIA

If you dull yourself by not eating, this also interferes with the energy and clarity you will need to recover from your misery addiction. Ask a doctor, HMO, hospital, psychologist, or other appropriate professional about a program that will help you get sufficient daily nutrition. Then work that program along with your misery addiction recovery program.

Abstinence in your case consists of eating three nutritious meals a day that provide at least the minimum daily caloric requirements for your body.

COMPULSIVE ACTIVITIES

The Activity Inventory chart will help you sort out how you're getting in your own way.

Please check all columns that apply. If a box is blacked out, leave it blank, but if it is gray or white, check it if it applies. The blacked-out boxes indicate usage is not problematic or does not fit that particular activity. If you aren't sure about the parameters of overdoing something, continue reading the rest of this chapter and then come back and complete the Activity Inventory chart.

If you checked three or more columns for any one activity, that activity is probably creating the kind of consequences that lead to misery. Put a star next to it in the left-hand margin.

Checking three or more gray boxes could indicate that you rotate among compulsive activities, using them interchangeably to avoid pain (and perhaps life). By itself one particular activity may not

Activity Inventory

Activity	2 or 3 times a day	Daily	2 or 3 times a week	Crave	Difficult to stop	Takes away time for living
Overworking	■					
Overexercising			■			
Internet surfing						
Computer games						
Excessive game-playing						
Too much or too little sleep	■					
Sacrificing yourself						
Caretaking others						
Gambling						
Obsessive cleaning						
Excessive television						
Compulsive eating						
Compulsive shopping						
Excessive tinkering						
Compulsive sexual activity						
Compulsive (fill in) _____						
Compulsive (fill in) _____						

reveal addictive involvement, but in concert with others you can
detect a pattern of avoidance or resistance. Put a star next to *each*
of these items in the left margin.

Now look at all of your starred activities. Using the Activity
Profile chart below, rate your starred activities according to preference, starting with 1 for your first choice, 2 for the activity you
turn to when number 1 isn't an option, and so on through your
personal list.

Activity Profile

Preference	Usage	Degree of interference	Activity
			Overworking
			Overexercising
			Internet surfing
			Computer games
			Excessive game-playing
			Too much or too little sleep
			Sacrificing yourself
			Caretaking others
			Gambling
			Obsessive cleaning
			Excessive television
			Compulsive eating
			Compulsive shopping
			Excessive tinkering
			Compulsive sexual activity
			Compulsive (fill in) _____
			Compulsive (fill in) _____

Next, rate your list according to usage. On the Activity Profile chart, place a 1 by the activity you do or use the most, a 2 by the activity you turn to next often for soothing or escape, and so on.

Finally, use the same chart to rate each of your activities by the degree to which they interfere with your life, starting with a number 1 by the activity that causes the most havoc or distress.

Now pick the top three items (numbers 1 to 3) from your interference list. These will be the compulsive activities you will work with first.

Next, fill in the boxes of the Tool Addiction Profile chart. List any substance addictions in box 1 and the top three activity addictions in box 2.

Tool Addiction Profile

Substance addictions	1.

Activity addictions	2. a.
	
	   b.
	
	   c.

	3. Self-sabotage

Your first goal is to achieve abstinence from all of the items you listed in the Tool Addiction Profile, including self-sabotage.

If this task seems overwhelming, congratulations! You've tapped into your powerlessness. Recognizing your true powerlessness will save you a lot of time and heartache.

Turn back to chapter 22 and read it with this list in mind. Perhaps now it is possible for you to honestly say, "I admit I am powerless over my addictions, and my life has become unmanageable."

Remember, for a challenge as large as recovering from a misery addiction, you'll need help. Consider going to a Twelve Step meeting this very week—perhaps even today. Visit the Misery Addicts Anonymous Web site (www.miseryaddicts.org) too, and attend one of its online meetings.

DEFINING ABSTINENCE

Abstinence means refraining from the substance or activity to which you are addicted. With some activities, such as food addiction, total abstinence is, of course, neither possible nor advised.

Focused recovery programs—most of them Twelve Step programs—have been established for many of these addictions. Check the phone book, a list of community resources at your library, and the Web for specific information. Appendix C of this book lists the parent organizations for many of these areas of recovery.

If you have multiple addictions, MAA (www.miseryaddicts.org) is one of your resources. MAA may stand for Misery Addicts Anonymous, but anyone with multiple addictions is also welcome.

Not sure whether you're doing or using something too much? Read and ponder the pages that follow.

Overworking

Abstinence consists of not overworking or not working compulsively.

This includes not volunteering excessively for extra work or extra responsibilities.

Volunteering out of enthusiasm and interest to coach the company softball team or plan the annual holiday party shows enthusiasm for the company. Being the primary volunteer most of the time for most things while your personal life suffers means that some internal impulse is pulling you out of balance.

If your job requires or expects you to work overtime—an increasingly common problem in many industries—then it's very important to begin setting limits about just how much overtime you will put in. If you typically work sixty hours a week, start by trimming away two hours each week. Next month, reclaim a couple of more hours weekly. Use these rescued hours to give yourself or your family the most benefit.

If doing this will give you a bad rap with your supervisor, talk to her about the need for more balance in your life, for the sake of your health. If there's an occasional push toward the end of a project where you need to work those extra hours again for a short while, that's fine—but be sure to return to the reduced hours as soon as the project is finished.

Those of us who are self-employed are vulnerable to working long hours because there's a direct correlation between hours worked and income. We may push ourselves too far out of fear that famine lurks beyond the next corner. But if you've made a living through self-employment for some years, you know that when you have energy, your business often increases, and when you get too tired, your business usually falls off. You can trust that you'll have what you need.

Some people overwork because they are perfectionists. This is a very common trait in addicts. They take six hours perfecting the chart they drew in twenty minutes, with corrections so minor that no one else notices them. Letting go of perfectionism is one of the challenges of recovery.

Your therapist or recovery group can also help you define abstinence from overwork. Then admit you are powerless over overworking; surrender and turn your work over to your Higher Power.

Overexercising

Exercise is good. Exercising three to five times a week for thirty to sixty minutes is excellent. An hour every day (excluding incidental exercise such as walking to work or playing basketball for fun) is a reasonable maximum. More exercise than that is excessive, unless you are an athlete in training for competition. For those of us not in training, abstinence consists of staying within the one-hour-a-day limit.

Internet Surfing

If you need to use the Internet for education, research, work, or shopping (provided you don't have a shopping compulsion), fine. A line gets crossed, however, if you sit at the computer for hours each day, following one link after another in an endless chain of self-stimulation. A line also gets crossed if you while away your time in chat rooms or fantasy Web sites, getting involved with e-mails to lots of people you don't even know, while at meals your friends or family stare at the empty chair where you used to sit.

If you want to use the Internet, do, but set an alarm for one hour. When the alarm beeps, leave the computer promptly. If just being online triggers an addictive response and you can't leave after an hour, find the information you need the old-fashioned way, at the library (but not through its computers) or through the Yellow

Pages. In your case abstinence will consist of giving up the Internet entirely, except in a controlled work environment.

MAA is your main resource.

Excessive Card or Computer Game-Playing

Playing solitaire compulsively or a Game Boy or other computer games for hours at a time, especially when you are shirking ordinary responsibilities or important interactions with others, is compulsive.

Try a modified form of abstinence by setting an alarm for one hour and leaving the game behind *promptly* when the alarm sounds, even (in fact, *especially*) if you're still in the middle of a round. If you can't leave, then your abstinence will have to consist of not playing games on the device at all.

Gamblers Anonymous and MAA are your best resources.

Too Much Sleep

On average, human beings need seven to nine hours of sleep each night. As we get older, the time needed may decrease or get partly redistributed into naps. Some people do need more sleep than others, however.

Excessive sleeping can be a sign of depression or seasonal affective disorder. Check with your doctor to see if you have other symptoms of either disorder.

In your heart you know if you are truly crawling into bed to avoid life. In this case, limit your sleep time gradually. Wake up earlier (first by half an hour, then by an hour or ninety minutes) and walk in the park, or stay up later and fill your evenings with good friends or a new hobby.

Your abstinence will consist of limiting your sleep to a reasonable number of hours—usually no more than nine per day.

Too Little Sleep

If you use an alarm to awaken, you are ending your rest before your body is ready to awaken. Ideally, you should be going to bed early enough that you rise naturally.

To be responsible, we set an alarm so that we can be sure to get to work on time—but if you are getting enough sleep, you will awaken on your own before the alarm sounds.

If, on the days you don't use an alarm, you sleep about a half hour longer, you are in the ballpark of being good to your body. On the other hand, if you sleep hours longer on your nonalarm days, you are operating in a sleep-deprived state the rest of the time.

Depriving yourself of sleep is serious. It can cause disordered eating, distortions of thinking, excessive reactiveness, and paranoia. You need a certain number of hours of sleep for your body to replenish itself and for your brain to reorganize itself.

Not sleeping enough is outright self-sabotage. From this decreased clarity, you can't make good decisions for yourself. You set yourself up to overeat and to create conflicts in your relationships.

Too much caffeine or chemical stimulation (whether in the form of cola, tea, coffee, smoking, or chocolate) can cause sleep difficulties. Stop all caffeine after noon. Train yourself to increase your sleep periods by adding fifteen minutes of sleep nightly for one week; then add additional fifteen-minute segments week after week until you no longer need your alarm.

Too little sleep, like too much sleep, can also be a sign of depression. Talk to your doctor to see if you have other symptoms of depression.

Abstinence consists of giving yourself enough sleep so that you don't need your alarm more than twice a week.

Self-Sacrificing and Caretaking

How do you know if you're giving away too much of yourself? Answer these questions:

1. When you have a need that competes with someone else's, are you likely to ignore yours for the sake of the other person's? Mothers and other primary caregivers of small children, bless your hearts, ignore this question. Come back to it in ten years.
2. Do you automatically sacrifice yourself for the people around you?
3. After you've let someone else go first, is it difficult to speak up and take your turn?
4. When helping or supporting someone else, do you often let your own preferences slide out of sight?

5. Do you find yourself surrounded by selfish people?

6. Are you afraid of being perceived as being selfish?

A "yes" to three or more of these questions probably indicates excessive self-sacrifice and caretaking.

This has deeper roots than most other compulsions. Self-sacrificing and caretaking can be major coping systems that have given you a ticket into relationships and become a part of your identity. You probably sacrifice automatically and may not even be conscious that you are doing it half the time.

Start here: for one week don't volunteer to do anything. Don't offer to help; don't take on a job that someone else has trouble doing. Notice how it feels. Then talk about your experience with a trustworthy friend.

Therapy will help get at the roots of this. The Twelve Step groups Al-Anon and Co-Dependents Anonymous can both help a great deal as well. Group therapy can teach you important new skills—especially saying no.

Abstinence in your case consists of making careful, considered decisions about when, how, and how much to offer to others. It means, at least for a while, never sacrificing yourself, your time, your energy, your dreams, your schedule, or your loved ones except in rare, dire circumstances. Once you break your pattern of caretaking, it might be possible to relax your stance on this—after talking over exceptions with your sponsor or therapist to be sure you aren't slipping into relapse.

The next exercise on self-knowledge will help.

— Exercise 5: Self-Knowledge —

1. Write down your own definitions of the following terms, then check the dictionary:

Column 1	Column 2
Self-centered	Self-awareness
Arrogant	Self-possession
Self-important	Self-assured

What are the differences between the meanings of the words in the first column as compared to the words in the second column?

2. Write down your answers to the following questions:

- How would you define selfishness?
- Who taught you to be afraid of being selfish?
- What lessons did they use to teach you this?
- Were you shamed for taking care of yourself? How?

After you've written about these things, look over your answers, think about them for a bit, and then talk about them with a trustworthy friend or therapist.

— —

Gambling

Gambling becomes compulsive when it results in more than minor financial losses, a wounded credit rating, or negative consequences for your family members, work, or health. If you find yourself manipulating others, lying, or craving to gamble, consider yourself a gambling addict.

Abstinence in your case consists of not gambling, betting, or wagering on anything and avoiding slippery places like racetracks, casinos, bingo halls, and lottery counters. Gamblers Anonymous is your recovery program and your best resource.

Obsessive Cleaning

This doesn't sound too serious until you talk to the children of obsessive cleaners who grew up thinking that the furniture was far more important than they were. Cleaning and straightening are necessary to keep our homes orderly, safe, and healthy. However, cleaning becomes compulsive when family members or guests can't relax because of your tidying or cleaning, or when a house isn't allowed to be lived in, or when your loved ones see you scurrying around cleaning instead of interacting with them.

Abstinence in your case consists of putting a time limit on tidying (set an alarm and obey it), restricting dusting to once a day, and vacuuming no more than twice a week (unless you have a pet with long hair or an allergic person in the household). It means letting a dish soak in the sink until the next meal is cleaned up and waiting for a full load before starting the dishwasher or washing machine.

In other words, abstinence consists of shifting your consciousness from an attempt at total control over your environment to more fluid aspects of life, such as productive activities and relationships.

If you compulsively clean your own body—e.g., take multiple showers every day or wash your hands over and over throughout the day—you could have obsessive-compulsive disorder, which now can be treated medically.

Some people who have experienced sexual abuse compulsively clean their bodies. If you have had to endure sexual abuse, you deserve more than scraping your skin off; you deserve the balm of therapy, which will bring you far deeper and longer-lasting relief than soap and water ever can.

Excessive Television

At what point does television watching get compulsive? When I ran this question by my friends, the answer was, "An hour more than I watch it."

As with most compulsions, the most telltale sign is the consequence of your use. Are you missing social activities with people you care about? Are you neglecting your need for rest, sleep, or quietude? Are your responsibilities being neglected? Are you exercising enough? Do you find yourself channel surfing late into the night, watching programs you aren't even interested in? All of these are signs of TV addiction.

Some TV addicts are addicted to one type of program but not others. Sports, soap operas, news programs, and reality shows each have their devotees. (I've been surprised to discover how many people feel they watch too much TV and keep it a secret, as if it is shameful.)

A good plan of modified abstinence would be setting a firm time to turn the TV off and enlisting the support of others to help you keep your promise to yourself. For example, you could promise yourself you will watch only your favorite two programs and commit to calling a friend and pressing the off button during the second set of credits. If that doesn't work, try totally abstaining from the category of programs you watch to excess but continuing to view programs you aren't compulsive about.

To keep from cheating yourself out of sleep and getting caught at midnight with the remote fused to your hand, try recording your favorite five shows each week and watching them all at once during a set time on the weekend.

Regardless of your brand of TV addiction, the way to push the off button is to get the support of others until it gets easy. It's also important to replace the dark set with interesting, productive activities.

If modified abstinence fails, then giving away your TV may be the only way to rescue your hours.

MAA is your main resource. Talking to a trusted friend, therapist, or sponsor can also help.

Compulsive Eating

Most compulsive eaters are also addicted to specific foods that trigger excessive eating. For these folks, the best way out is through abstinence from the addictive foods.

Some people, however, can be abstinent from trigger foods and still overeat the remaining foods in the spectrum. If this describes you, then your abstinence consists of three defined meals a day, sometimes with one or two additional, clearly defined snack times. Reasonable portions should be weighed and measured.

It is difficult to stay clean on such a program without a sponsor and multiple recovery meetings every week. Overeaters Anonymous (OA), HOW (which stands for Honesty, Openness, Willingness, a more structured type of OA meeting), and Food Addicts Anonymous are all helpful resources.

Compulsive Shopping

You have a compulsive shopping problem if you shop to take a break from other compulsions, use shopping to avoid feeling pain, spend money that was earmarked for necessities, buy things you don't need, take bags home and never take the purchases out, or have credit problems as a result of your shopping.

Modified abstinence here could consist of setting time limits for shopping, buying only what's on a previously prepared list, requiring a call to your sponsor for any purchase over fifty dollars, shopping only with a conscious friend, and staying out of stores and shopping centers at all other times. Create boundaries around garage sales and street fairs by going without a checkbook or credit card, carrying only a twenty-dollar bill in your pocket.

Total abstinence from shopping can be arranged, if necessary, by paying someone else to do it.

MAA is your best resource.

Excessive Tinkering

This is a catchall category for any activity that you do so often or compulsively that it interferes with your participation in the good things of life. It could mean spending too much time with your head under the hood of a car, sewing compulsively, or rearranging your living room twice a week.

If you aren't sure whether you are doing something compulsively, poll your friends and family. They'll know.

A trusted person in recovery can help you figure out a realistic program of abstinence. Whether your abstinence can be modified or must be total depends on the degree to which the activity interferes with the rest of your life and on how well you can sustain that moderated level over time.

MAA is your main resource.

Compulsive Sexual Activity

Sex addiction gives a vivid glimpse into the progressive nature of addiction. Starting, for example, with excessive self-stimulation through touch or preoccupation with pornographic materials, a sex addict soon tires of the current level of stimulation and seeks some sort of increase—through more vivid materials, through riskier situations, or through an increasing number or variety of sexual partners.

A sex addict may have one sexual behavior or obsession that troubles him, or many. Possible aspects can be abuse of yourself, abuse of others, lying, secrecy, conflictual relationships, unwanted pregnancies, exposure to disease, and breaking the law. The behaviors of sex addiction can bring feelings of shame, self-loathing, and hopelessness.

Under the influence of a sexual addiction, moral boundaries can be crossed. A sex addict may break promises of fidelity to a mate. He may manipulate another person to get what he needs. He may misuse his position of power or authority. She may put herself in dangerous situations. She may enter liaisons with people who can hurt her. She may expose herself to arrest or disease.

How can you tell when a normal level of sexual interest crosses the line into addiction? Ask yourself these questions:

- Am I obsessed with sex? Does it intrude on my thoughts when I am trying to focus on work or social activities?
- Has my involvement progressed?
- Have I exposed myself to danger—through illness or harmful people?
- Am I doing things sexually that cause me shame?
- Am I doing things in secret, barely admitting even to myself what I am doing?
- Have I told myself I would stop doing a certain thing and then gone back to doing it many times again?
- Have I lost someone important to me because of my sexual activities?
- Are my finances stretched because of my sexual activities?
- Have I lost interest in nonsexual aspects of living?

A healthy sexual relationship with a loved one or a respected mate is a joyous experience. Sexual exploration and experimentation in that context can be delightful.

It's when the pursuit of sexual experience takes over your life, creating an increasing pile of problematic consequences, that you have a bright signal of the need for help.

Abstinence includes refraining from participation in sexual activities that are harmful or dangerous (to yourself or others) and that endanger your marriage, professional position, or finances. It includes eliminating exposure to sexual stimulation that triggers your cravings. Further refinements on abstinence can be defined with the help of a sponsor.

If you suffer from this, there's a strong possibility you were abused sexually. Certain programs and therapists specialize in programs for abusers, offenders, and victims.

Your best resources are Sex and Love Addicts Anonymous and Sex Addicts Anonymous. Both have Web sites with tests you can use to privately assess yourself. (You can find the Web addresses in appendix C.)

Self-Sabotage

Self-sabotage is *the* essential behavior of misery addiction. It can take an almost infinite number of forms, such as lateness; breaking promises; not showing up; not preparing; projecting old issues onto people and events in the present; making assumptions and acting on them as if they were a reality; not expressing your needs; expecting others to read your mind; sacrificing yourself for others; suppressing your feelings; caretaking others; not acting when action is needed; chasing away the people who could help; taking poor care of yourself; sabotaging friendships; not taking effective medication; using tool addictions; and avoiding important people, events, and feelings.

Abstinence here requires mindfulness because there are so many ways to sabotage oneself. Therefore, the first tier of abstinence from self-sabotage is to abstain from anything that dulls or alters your consciousness. This means that you need to get enough sleep, sufficient nutrition, appropriate medication (if needed), and reasonable exercise. You also need to avoid mind-dulling activities and substances such as television, computer game-playing, sugar, and alcohol.

Self-sabotage is insidious. It has a thousand ways to snare you. The tool addictions will put pressure on you to return to your old habits, sending out their seductive sirens whenever you falter in your program. Regular, consistent support, daily working the first three Steps, and the Daily Practice described below are your best protection against being shanghaied.

– Daily Practice –

Morning

When you first wake up, repeat the first three Steps aloud:

1. We admitted we were powerless over self-sabotage—that our lives had become unmanageable.

2. Came to believe that a Power greater than ourselves could restore us to sanity.
3. Made a decision to turn our will and our lives over to the care
   of God as we understood God. (Substitute "Higher Power" for
   "God" if you like.)

Next, look at your plan for the day. Look for those events, appointments,
obligations, plans, or places that could seduce you to sabotage yourself.

1. Your schedule:
   a. Is it too full?
      i. Will you have trouble getting meals in?
      ii. What can you reschedule?
   b. Is it too empty?
      i. Call your sponsor.
      ii. Go to a meeting.
   c. Are you prepared to carry out all of your responsibilities?
   d. *Realistically,* when do you need to leave for each appoint-
      ment, event, or meeting in order to be at least five minutes
      early, even if traffic is worse than usual?
2. Think about where, when, and how you will get your meals.
3. Plan and schedule at least one rest period in your day. This
   should be at least half an hour.
4. Plan for a meeting or a call with a healthy friend or your
   sponsor.
5. Ask yourself: Is there anything about my day that needs to be
   changed to protect my abstinence?

As your day proceeds, if you have an impulse to do something you
haven't planned or to sacrifice something good that you have scheduled, ask yourself this vital question: Am I thinking of doing this because I'm addicted to misery?

Evening

Keep a notebook by your bed. Before you go to sleep each night (and
before you get too tired), mentally review your day. Respond to or do
the following:

1. What part of the day went beautifully? What pattern did you follow that made it so?
2. What part of the day fell apart? What planning, action, or decision could have created a better outcome?
3. What can you learn about your pattern from what happened? What can you learn from it about yourself?
4. In your notebook, jot down what you learned. Convert all mistakes to lessons.
5. Quickly write down three things you are grateful for.
6. Put your arms around yourself and give yourself comfort. Picture these as the arms of someone who loves you. If someone else who loves you is beside you (or nearby), ask to spend some time in this person's arms as well.
7. Go to sleep early enough to get sufficient rest for the next day.

An unwillingness to do this Daily Practice indicates that your recovery is out of whack. Whenever you don't want to do the Daily Practice, go to a recovery meeting ASAP, or call your sponsor promptly.

CHAPTER TWENTY-SIX

Now That I'm Recovering I'm Feeling Stuff

Okay. Hold on. This can turn out all right.

Having feelings is a good sign. It means your recovery is working.

As you move into right relationship with your feelings, they'll show up in a rich palette that both informs you and gives dimension to your world. Your full range of feelings, allowed to do their job, will pick up the delicate undercurrents in your various relationships, the subtle energies floating around the people you are with, and your reaction to those energies.

As your recovery proceeds, feelings may start getting jammed shoulder to shoulder, like two people caught in a door as they try to leave at the same time. It will take a while to get the backlog sorted out. Plan to be uncomfortable for a while. Give yourself six months to learn how to feel and to get used to it.

Handling your feelings well is your number one protection against relapse. If at any point you have a subtle, stuck feeling, it is generally the first tug that, if unaddressed, will start a downward slide.

When we are inside an addiction, we are not in right relationship with our feelings. The addiction erects a barrier between knowing and feeling, and it alters our consciousness.

Practicing misery addicts generally have two types of distortion messing up their contact with their feelings: (1) a few feelings are running the show and (2) the rest of the palette of emotions is being suppressed. This causes a misery addict to have pretty much the same reaction to everything he encounters.

Benjamin reacted with anger to everything. He saw what was missing instead of what was good in a situation. If his wife bought his favorite butter peas, he was angry because she didn't buy his favorite type of seasoning to go with it. His own responsibility in setting up that situation—never describing to her the type of seasoning he preferred—was invisible to him.

Melva got victimized at the drop of a cap. A teenager (speeding three lanes away) feeling his oats by banging on his horn at other young four-wheeled bucks, sent Melva into gyrations of meekness. If a stranger cursed over the crack in the sidewalk, Melva apologized and felt responsible.

This single, overused feeling—anger for Benjamin and Melva's feeling of being responsible for everything—blots out the subtler nuances and maintains a running internal monologue that pushes a misery addict's interactions in the same general direction, regardless of what's really happening.

Kali Rose cycled among rage, shame, and self-sacrificing adoration. Helena lived inside a storm of self-blame, with an occasional deluge of shame. Ingrid, focused primarily outside herself, felt the feelings of others instead of her own.

When we narrow ourselves down to a few feelings, they can become greatly amplified. Thus if anger is our main feeling, we are often vulnerable to rage. If sadness is number one, then despair is likely. Anxiety becomes fear, and fear turns into terror. Loneliness expands to abandonment and desolation.

We feel before we think—yet we can avoid a feeling so quickly after it strikes us that it's buried before we recognize it. This untimely burial, faster than anything else, sends the misery addict to one of her tool addictions. (One service and disservice of any addiction is that it tends to bury all traces of feeling.)

Feelings are felt; they aren't thought. Yes, this is stating the obvious. But the significance of this is that feelings, unlike thoughts, will tell you your genuine reaction to something, if you let them. Feelings always carry information—truthful information that goes deeper than thought. Feelings can't lie.

However, feelings don't always reflect the truth about the current situation. A current situation can be confused with something from your past. Thus your feeling can relay a truth about a memory rather than about what's happening right now. Remember the case of the woman for whom the rotating fan at an exercise club brought up feelings about the death and disappearance of her mother?

By allowing yourself to feel your feelings all the way through to their unfolding, you will discover whether they're really about now or about the past. Then you can determine what action is appropriate.

But if you cut off your feelings or put all of your feelings in one basket, you will have trouble distinguishing details in the present from those of the past, and you run the risk of reacting inappropriately.

Stanton was standing at the door, his face puzzled. "Do you want to go in your car?"

Maris tried to hold on to her patience. "I said, 'Let's go in *your* car.' Why is this so hard?"

"Do you mean my current car or the car you drive that used to be mine?"

Maris's tone was ugly. "Stanton, we stopped calling the car I drive yours six months ago. Let's. Go. In. Your. *Green*. Car!"

He looked very hurt and ducked through the door.

Maris felt bad immediately, but the trouble with hurtful words is that the sting can't be taken back. She thought about why she'd gotten angry so fast. This time she let herself feel her fury again, but without involving Stanton. As she allowed herself to fully feel her anger, she realized she was annoyed with one of his traits. He was a very good man, but he sometimes got simple logistics confused, especially when pronouns were involved.

She felt shame, then, because she knew simple confusion wasn't worth venom.

Then she made herself go back to the process and feel still more deeply into the anger. At once she was transported back in time.

"Maris, I don't want to be alone," whined her fifty-year-old mother. "Please let me come with you and your friends." Though it was inappropriate and would change the caliber of the evening, thirty-year-old Maris gave in and succumbed to her mother's manipulation.

Maris recalled another moment from the past. "Maris, don't tell anyone he attacked you. Okay?" Her mother kept her eyes forward as she drove, not reaching out in any way to Maris after she'd been mauled by a filthy drunk in the school parking lot as she waited for her tardy mother. And thirteen-year-old Maris felt even sicker.

Then another memory was triggered. "Oh, don't give her anything. She doesn't need anything," said her mother brightly after dragging six-year-old Maris to an adult party without warning the hostess. Maris was hungry and thirsty, not having eaten since her school lunch, but she sat quietly at the side of the room for the rest of the party.

Maris came back to the present enlightened. Stanton had not deserved her ire. By letting herself feel her anger *apart from him,* her memories helped her understand the pattern. Her anger was about bearing the brunt of someone else's condition. In the half minute Stanton got confused about the cars, she was put into the position of straightening things out for him. With Stanton, whom she loved deeply, this was indeed a small thing.

With her mother, however, this had been a gigantic thing. Her mother's self-absorption and dependence had often landed Maris in situations where she was sacrificed for her mother's needs. Her anger belonged not toward Stanton, but toward her mother, Drusilla.

Maris had been triggered by a pattern. The pattern was subtle, and the current event did not warrant the strength of her reaction. But by allowing herself to feel more deeply, she uncovered the pattern and understood the buried anger that had been activated by the current situation.

Further work on the pattern allowed her to see what was lost in those and many other interactions with her mother—her own reality. Even after the extreme circumstances of Maris being mauled by a drunk, Drusilla could not come out of her self-absorption to offer comfort to her daughter. She thought only of how it would affect her and talked Maris into keeping quiet about the incident in order to spare herself the trouble of making a police report. (She may also have been trying to avoid being seen as an inadequate parent, one who was unable to protect her daughter from harm.)

Maris's reality was invisible to Drusilla, and Drusilla's obtuseness made Maris's reality unclear to herself as well. As an adult in recovery, Maris fought tooth and nail for her reality whenever it was threatened, especially when it was threatened by obtuseness—hence the strength of her reaction to Stanton.

Uncovering this allowed Maris to shift. She immediately began working her program to eliminate targeting Stanton unfairly and did some anger work about her mother to air out that closet of hurt.

Her feelings were appropriate for the past. They were inappropriate in the present. Had she just buried her feelings of shame and true remorse at hurting Stanton, she would have lost two things: a way to transform her shame into something useful and the key to an issue that popped up with Stanton regularly but, in fact, belonged to the past.

Once she knew where the problem truly lay, she could direct her work toward this unfinished business. She also understood the deep importance of honoring her own reality and began gathering tools to protect her reality in ways that wouldn't hurt anyone else. In fact, the work she did transformed her relationship with Stanton. She stopped having to make herself be patient and was able to see him as he truly was—kind and present, not anything like her mother.

The past can blind us to the present. Misery addicts suffer from this frequently as they try to fend off feelings and hurts that occurred long ago, unknowingly dispersing the good that is trying to reach them right now. The way we free ourselves from such bondage is to allow feelings to go all the way to the bottom.

Abstinence from your addictions takes away the padding that has been swaddling your feelings. For perhaps the first time in years, you have an opportunity to work with yourself in a way that will clean out the closets of your past. This takes a lot of courage—but you have this courage because you got yourself into recovery and started changing your life.

Feelings can seem enormous and endless, as if they'll swallow you up and go on forever. In fact, the more you open yourself to the fullness of a feeling, the more quickly it will pass. They only

have that sense of endlessness when they are being blocked or de-
nied. Then they pop up indirectly all over the place.

A HEALTHY FEELING PROCESS

The process of feeling, if allowed to flow fully and freely, proceeds
in a predictable fashion:

1. An event takes place.
   a. An event triggers the feeling. That event can be inter-
      nal (something inside you) or external.
   b. The trigger may not be obvious.
2. A feeling begins.
   a. It can pop up suddenly and powerfully.
   b. It can sneak in unannounced.
   c. It can show up as a mere shift in mood.
   d. You may not be sure what event caused this reaction.
3. You attend to the feeling.
   a. You shift your attention to your inner self.
   b. You allow yourself to clearly experience the feeling.
      This is the part that requires your willingness and your
      mindful attention.
   c. You continue to fully experience the feeling, without
      judgment or filtering.
4. The feeling amplifies and becomes more intense.
5. You help the feeling amplify.
   a. You scan your body to see where your feeling is located
      most strongly, e.g.
      • a knot in your stomach
      • a tight throat
      • a hollow heart
      • clenched jaws
   b. You put your hand on the place of greatest intensity.
   c. You breathe deeply into that place.
6. The feeling sharpens.
   a. You are almost through it. Knowing this, you do not run
      from the feeling but ride it as it sharpens.

   b. You remind yourself that this is like the bite right before the tooth comes out or the prick right before the pimple bursts.
 7. You express the feeling.
   a. You make sounds. "Ohhhh."
   b. You use words. "It hurts. It feels like I'm being crushed."
   c. You describe internal images. "It's like a huge fiery ball."
   d. You let yourself move. "My hands want to shake. I'll let them."
 8. You go with what happens next.
   a. You may be given a memory. "I'm suddenly remembering the day my father lost his job."
   b. You may be given a picture. "I can see my mother's face."
   c. You may see a pattern. "That's just like what my brother would say to me."
   d. You may be given information. "She didn't want children. It isn't personal."
 9. You keep going with what happens.
   a. "And now I'm remembering . . ."
   b. "This is the story coming to me."
   c. "I just want to beat on the couch." (Go ahead as long as nobody gets hurt.)
10. The feeling diminishes or suddenly disappears. In its place a need may appear. Address that need if you can, or ask someone else to help.
   a. "Well, I'm thirsty."
   b. "I feel different."
   c. "Will you hold me?"
11. You rest.
   a. You allow the flow of further feelings and insights.
   b. You let yourself be comforted.
   c. You let yourself feel the peace of understanding.
   d. You notice the new feeling and perhaps either a comfortable tiredness or a burst of energy.

From beginning to end, the entire process usually takes no more than twenty minutes, and often much less, if you don't fight it. For something huge, it can take a couple of hours but rarely more than that.

A devastating event, such as the death of a loved one, may cause you to walk this road many times over several months. For ordinary life situations, however, the entire process can be fairly quick, especially as you get better at sticking with it from beginning to end. (The more you resist or block or try to avoid the process, the longer it will take.)

If you are a misery addict, you probably didn't have a parent helping you with your feelings, which is why you never learned what to do with them. By taking your feelings through the above process, you parent yourself most kindly.

Since feelings may be frightening at first—until you can begin trusting that they will pass—it helps to practice these steps for the first fifty times with some other kind and wise soul, such as a therapist, sponsor, or friend in recovery.

After you've been through the feeling process, comfort feels really wonderful if you can let yourself have it. Comfort balms the body and soothes the soul. Letting yourself be quietly held for twenty minutes by someone who cares for you can be truly heavenly.

However, *misplaced* comfort can interfere with the process. If someone tries to comfort you while you're still at step four, for example, you need to stop this person, or you'll get cut off just as you're about to bear fruit.

Our number one reason for any addiction is changing how we feel. But if we can allow ourselves to feel our feelings, then we have far less reason to turn to the addiction.

WHAT TO DO IF YOU DON'T FEEL ANYTHING

After a lifetime of avoiding feelings, yours may be buried very deep. To tap into them again, arrange some quiet times with a therapist or a recovering friend. Prime the pump by thinking of a time during the previous week when you had a negative reaction to somebody, such as irritation or sadness.

Use that experience as your material as you follow the steps in the feeling process, verbalizing each step.

Practicing this once a day will help you open up and discover your real self.

This sounds scary, I know. This whole process flies in the face of how you've painstakingly arranged your entire life.

But it will be more than worth it. It will enable you to make the transition from numbness to joy. You will at last be able to engage in your own life.

WHAT TO DO IF YOU FEEL TOO MUCH

When you take the cap off the volcano, of course it will blow. Down the road a piece, this will naturally calm down.

A woman who has blocked anger her whole life may be quite angry at almost everything and everyone for a couple of months. But the storm will blow over.

However, if anger is the feeling that comes out, remember to direct it away from anyone who might be hurt by it. If you need to, curse or scream or beat up a pillow in private. In particular, keep your release of anger away from children. (Remember how Maris put boundaries around her anger and, after the first instance, worked with her anger only after Stanton was out of the room.)

If grief is the feeling that comes out, find a comforting friend or therapist to talk to. Allow yourself to accept the soothing and concern your friend or therapist gives.

WHAT TO DO WHEN YOU'RE FEELING VULNERABLE

We feel exposed when we finally start living without our insulation. Unlike in childhood, however, you now have resources. When you feel vulnerable, you have some choices.

- You can take it through the full feeling process.
- You can ask for and receive comfort from others.
- You can think your way through it, remembering the resources you have now.

WHAT TO DO IF YOU FEEL SCARED—
PERHAPS EVEN ALL OF THE TIME

Fear is just a feeling—no more and no less. Take it through the feeling process, and as much as possible, spend time with your recovery community. If you feel afraid all of the time, you are tapping
into something real that frightened you at an earlier time. There is
a cause, and if you are around safe people long enough, you will
let yourself know what it is.

In recovery we need to let people love us until we can love ourselves. We have to let ourselves be sheltered by safe people until
we can find our own strength.

Sometimes, as we go deeper inside, we may come to the edge of
an abyss, and we know instinctively that if we go down there, we
will discover that something very bad happened.

Is it essential to discover the details? Not necessarily. It can be
enough just to know that something bad happened. We can make
this work by letting ourselves have all the feelings around it. We
let ourselves have feelings about the bad event, without identifying what was so bad about it. We let the feelings be the evidence.
We trust them and allow the process to work. This can be sufficient
and allow us to move on.

YIKES! I'M FEELING HAPPY

Steady now. It's going to be okay. This doesn't have to be a bad
thing.

Sooner or later (usually sooner) in your recovery, happiness will
appear. It may completely frighten you.

Your fear is about the past, remember, not the present. Something in the past made you scared of being happy. Something bad
probably happened after you felt good.

You knew this would happen, but you're still afraid. What do
you do? Try these ideas:

- Change the pattern. Instead of letting anxiety about happiness create a setup for pain, set up some good right now.
  Make plans to do something you love, either alone or
  (preferably) with someone you like being with.

- Build a new pattern by rewarding yourself for feeling happy. Think of something simple (and easily obtainable) that you would enjoy right now. Then do it—also right now.
- Review and repeat the first three Steps of the Twelve Steps (see appendix A).
- Take this combination of fear and happiness back through the feeling process. It will link you to the internal place where joy and loss got bonded together. Doing this work back in your personal history will begin to change your emotional programming.
- Call a friend. Get encouragement for changing your life and reassurance that you deserve joy.
- Go to a Twelve Step (or other recovery) meeting.
- Look at the rest of your day and identify the places where you could set yourself up to give yourself some trouble. Resolve to do the opposite action (see Tool Belt on pages 228–229) in each of these situations so that the day goes well.
- Go to the next chapter, "Toolshed," and take out the mindfulness tool on page 216. Be fully present right now, in this moment. Anchor yourself in the present.

THE SPECIAL CASE OF SHAME

Guilt is the feeling we have when we've done something wrong. Shame is feeling wrong simply for existing. Often this translates into a deeply felt but unexplained feeling of worthlessness or unworthiness.

Shame is an implanted feeling. We do not naturally develop shame. It comes about because someone treated us in a shaming way.

Shame does not tell the truth about you. It tells a truth about someone else—the shamer.

The process for handling shame is different from the process for handling other feelings since this is an absorbed rather than an intrinsic feeling.

The person who said or did shaming things to you was actually trying to protect himself from something in his own world—most likely something in his inner world, something that was there long before you entered the scene. In shaming you, he sacrificed you for his need.

When we internalize that shame, we keep the process going. We continue protecting the shamer, sacrificing ourselves for her—often long after the shamer is dead or no longer in our life.

We can be shamed by words and by actions. If this happens enough, unworthiness can eventually become our core experience of ourselves.[1]

Unworthiness is at the root of self-sabotage. Deep inside, we feel undeserving of the goodness that could show up if we made efforts on our own behalf. We then set ourselves up for negative outcomes that match our sense of insignificance.

Some of the actions that can cause shame include the following:

- deliberate, unwanted physical (or sexual) contact, especially when you were young
- physical violence
- wisecracks directed at your physical attributes
- hurtful teasing
- touch that hurts, especially in intimate areas
- premature exposure to sexuality
- being given derogatory nicknames
- excessive or inappropriate punishment
- torture
- insults about your gender, race, religion, nationality, appearance, or personality
- inequitable distribution of favors
- critical remarks
- a negative response from someone when you've done a good thing
- a dismissive or negative response from someone when you tell him about your joy, achievement, or award

Being treated in such ways causes a sense of wrongness to grow inside of us. It's like kudzu or brambles growing inside our psyche, crowding out our self-esteem and well-being. With enough repetition, it eventually becomes part of our personal infrastructure, a part of who we are—and thus difficult to challenge.

Once it becomes your experience of yourself, it's more than a feeling. It becomes your identity. To challenge your feeling of shame then becomes a challenge to your identity.

HANDLING SHAME

When you experience shame, regardless of the immediate cause, ask yourself eleven questions to process the feeling.[2] Answer them however you like; feel your way into them. If possible, write down your answers.

The feeling of shame may have swelled because of something that happened today or because something today brought back an experience from the past. Whether the trigger is real or metaphorical, whether past or present, literal or figurative, use this process. It's also possible that the feeling arose suddenly, for no reason you can put your finger on. It's more important to feel into the questions than to think logically about them. These questions can be helpful in all of these cases.

Questions to Process Shame

1. How old do I feel?
2. What's happening that is increasing my sense of shame?
   a. Am I being yelled at? Am I yelling at myself internally?
   b. Am I being physically hurt? Am I hurting myself?
   c. Am I being ignored?
   d. Am I being unfairly criticized?
3. Who is doing this to me? Am I doing it to myself?
4. What are they doing that feels shaming? (Examples: the silent treatment, walking away, being disgusted with me, telling me I'm stupid or lazy)

continued on the next page

Questions to Process Shame *continued*

5. If someone else is doing this to me, what is that person protecting himself or herself from? If that person weren't focusing on me, what would he or she have to notice or feel instead?
6. Am I willing to stop protecting that person by not letting such maneuvers work?
7. Am I feeling shame because of something that person is not doing? What is communicated to me by that person's lack of action? What do I tell myself this means?
8. Am I able to realize that this person's shaming is really about him or her and not about me?
9. Am I willing to give up thinking of myself as worthless?
10. If I acknowledge this is about the other person and not me, what would my experience of myself be?
11. Am I willing to accept a shift in my identity?

After you've answered these questions, get in touch with a kind, accepting friend or someone else you can talk to who has a history of treating you with kindness and acceptance. (Don't pick anyone who has treated you in a shaming way or who may try to defend or excuse the shamer.) Ask this kind person to spend some time with you and just listen to you with compassion.

Establish the amount of time you both have for this process in advance so that you don't rush unnecessarily or suddenly have to stop. Find or create an environment that won't interrupt you. This should be in private rather than in a public place. Turn off phones. Don't have food nearby. (Food will distract you from feeling and may distract your companion from listening.)

As you sit with this kind person, talk about how you feel, and discuss your answers to the Questions to Process Shame. If you are both comfortable with doing so, touch in some way while you are talking. For example, hold hands, or sit so that your knees or shoulders touch. As you get more comfortable with each other, perhaps you can allow yourself to be held while you talk. If you begin (or want) to cry, let yourself.

Ideally, this process ends with being embraced kindly and lovingly and relaxing into the peacefulness of being cared for.

If involving another person is too difficult, start by embracing yourself as you answer the questions. Imagine that the arms around you are a loving grandmother or even an angel. Then talk out loud to this loving image about feeling ashamed or worthless.

If at any point in doing this process you come to a halt, unable to go all the way to the end, then your next task is to find a caring group or community—such as a good Twelve Step meeting—that will help you move from shame to release.

If someone in your present life is trying to shame you, protect yourself from being harmed by it. The next time he tries it, ask yourself this question: *To whose advantage is it that I believe what he is saying to me?* If your answer is "him," remember that you are not required to sacrifice your own serenity or self-esteem for anyone else. Instead, do one or more of the following:

1. Say, "I can't talk to you about this now."
2. Say, "Please talk about how *you* feel, not about what I *am*."
3. Use the techniques from chapter 27 to ask the person to stop saying shaming things to you.
4. Stop spending time with this person.

Shame can do a great deal of damage. It's an insidious influence that can hurl us backward. Use the above processes anytime your shame meter gets activated.

THE FLOW OF FEELING

Your inner self will direct your healing, if you let it, at its own wise pace. It will pluck out of the current environment the exact intimation that has the capacity of bringing forward whatever primeval issue is next on the healing agenda. For example, the incident with

Stanton was a signal to Maris that an inner closet had opened with artifacts to sort through. By clearing out those cluttered feelings, Maris became a notch freer and healthier.

A pivotal childhood event may carry a flock of issues—different aspects, different messages—that fly off now and then and need attention. A single event can send you repeatedly through the feeling process. This means that, in order to move completely through it, you may experience grief, sadness, denial, anger, and fear, in any order or combination. At times you might also feel embarrassment, loneliness, and/or excessive responsibility.

As you are using the feeling process, you won't necessarily visit each part a single time. Especially with a complex event, you may find yourself moving through parts two through nine multiple times before you are ready for the final steps.

This is both normal and appropriate. In fact, it is the path to freedom from your past.

CHAPTER TWENTY-SEVEN

Toolshed

It's okay to be laying down your tool addictions, because I have something better for you to use. Replace your tool addictions with tools that actually promote positive action and growth.

This chapter is your toolshed. Come back here to get a tool whenever a job gets too tough for bare hands.

An addict's typical response to new tools—when she's thinking with an addicted mind—is something like this:

- It's too simple. I'll dismiss it.
- It's too complex. I feel overwhelmed by it and can't begin to think of using it.

So tune in to the first three Steps for a moment to get yourself back into your recovering mind.

1. We admitted we were powerless over self-sabotage—that our lives had become unmanageable.
2. Came to believe that a Power greater than ourselves could restore us to sanity.
3. Made a decision to turn our will and our lives over to the care of God as we understood God.

Good. Like many of us, you've admitted that you need help. These tools help. They give you various ways to stay conscious and focused. And they can improve your mood so that you don't have to resort to any tool addictions or behaviors.

MINDFULNESS

Living mindfully brings you into consciousness of the good that is already surrounding you. You have the gift of a splendid day arrayed before you. Pause. Settle. Breathe. Take it in. Something within sight is beautiful, intricate, or meaningful.

You are alive right now. Focus into this one moment. You have everything you need in this moment.

Experience more right now. Be in the present. Following is an exercise from a helpful guide to mindfulness, *Peace Is Every Step.*[1]

— Exercise 6: Present Moment, Wonderful Moment —

Sitting in a comfortable position, say the following lines in coordination with breathing in and breathing out:

> *Breathing in, I calm my body.*
> *Breathing out, I smile.*
> *Dwelling in the present moment,*
> *I know this is a wonderful moment!*

After getting used to this sequence and letting the meaning percolate into your cells, shift into these lines:

> *Calming, smiling,*
> *Present moment, wonderful moment.*

No matter what else you may be feeling, stopping and being mindful takes you back into reality—the larger reality often obscured by your racing mental motor. In this moment, you have what you need. A bird is singing. The air is soft on your skin. We often think we need to suppress our anger, but Thich Nhat Hanh, a world authority on peace, has alternate advice. He writes:

> When our anger is placed under the lamp of mindfulness, it immediately begins to lose some of its destructive nature.

We can say to ourselves, "Breathing in, I know that anger is in me. Breathing out, I know that I am my anger." If we follow our breathing closely while we identify and mindfully observe our anger, it can no longer monopolize our consciousness.

When we are angry, we are not usually inclined to return to ourselves. We want to think about the person who is making us angry, to think about his hateful aspects. . . . The more we think about him, listen to him, or look at him, the more our anger flares . . . but, the root of the problem is the anger itself, and we have to come back and look first of all inside ourselves. . . . Like a fireman, we have to pour water on the blaze first and not waste time looking for the one who set the house on fire.

"Breathing in, I know that I am angry. Breathing out, I know that I must put all my energy into caring for my anger."

When we are angry, our anger is our very self. To suppress or chase it away is to suppress or chase away our self. When we are joyful, we are the joy. When we are angry, we are the anger.[2]

GROUNDING

Grounding gives roots to mindfulness by combining mindfulness with connection to the earth.

Grounding yourself is easy. Go outside and lean against a tree. Stand barefoot on the soil. Lie spread-eagle on the ground. Picture roots spreading out from your feet into the earth. Feel the life force of the tree or the soil.

This honors your physical body, the materials of which all came from the earth. Breathe the earth, drink the air, eat the sun.

BLAME VERSUS TRUTH

Addicts tend to blame themselves or others. Sadly, we have precious little control over the actions of our parents, mates, or bosses. We can set boundaries to stop them from hurting us, but we have no control over their choices or their ability to treat us fairly or kindly.

Misery addicts who sacrifice themselves routinely operate under this principle: "If I give you what you need, you will give me what I need from you." (In other words, "If I fill you up, you'll pour goodies back on me.") It's a fair and reasonable principle, but it's often 180 degrees from the truth. We could drench an angry or dependent parent or spouse with energy or love—for years or even decades—and get little or nothing back (or, worse, get back abuse). We don't want to face the fact that the tree is barren. But we won't get fruit from it no matter what we do.

In our disappointment that our sacrifice hasn't done us any good, we may express our anger by blaming—ourselves for wasting the effort or the other person for taking without giving back. Blame won't cause the person to give us anything, and blame won't give anything to us.

We have no power to get another person to feel his own feelings, handle his own issues, or change his values. We are powerless to force someone else to take in or appreciate what we have to offer.

Truth? Now that's another matter. Blaming and telling the truth are different species. Blame puts the focus on the other person. Truth observes the reality. Telling the truth lets you understand the other person, yourself, and your relationship.

Telling yourself the truth—which is a far different thing from blaming—allows you to stop squandering energy on someone who won't change. It is enormously helpful when you can admit to yourself, "No matter what I give her, she still won't understand me." "He was abusive—that's just the reality." In telling yourself the truth, you can stop yourself from watering a plant that will never bear fruit.

These principles also apply to the way you talk to yourself. Hanh wisely writes, "When you plant lettuce, if it does not grow well, you don't blame the lettuce. You look into the reasons it is not doing well."[3]

Blaming yourself for not having lived your life differently is like blaming lettuce for growing slowly. You grew as you did because of the way you were watered and fed.

Allow yourself to understand this. This is telling yourself the truth.

Now, realizing this, you can put your attention to giving *yourself* the nourishment you were looking to get from the barren tree by going to a different orchard where the trees are heavy with fruit (like a recovery meeting).

COMPASSIONATE COMMUNICATION

In his book *Nonviolent Communication*^{SM}*: A Language of Life, Marshall Rosenberg offers a powerful tool to improve our communication—not just with others, but with ourselves.

Learning this system gives you a different way to listen to others and greater clarity and competence in how you respond to them. It gives you protection from others' harmful communication, no matter how overt or subtle they may be about it, and it increases your odds of communicating in a way in which everyone is satisfied.

First, let's look at communication styles that aren't productive.

1. Moralistic judgments—akin to blaming or judging yourself or others as bad or wrong for not adhering to your principles.
2. Making comparisons—comparing your body, your choices, your achievements, your car, and your toothpaste to those of others. Paying a lot of attention to how a boss, parent, or friend treats peers as compared to you.
3. Denying personal responsibility—looking at a situation in terms of the other person's mistakes instead of taking inventory of your own part in the outcome.
4. Demanding—demands invite resistance, even when you make a demand of yourself. A demand embeds force, and no one likes to be forced.

---

* Service mark for the Center for Nonviolent Communication (www.cnvc.org).

Here are the components of compassionate communication:

1. observation
2. feeling
3. needs
4. request

This structure can be used both for the way you express something to another person and for the consciousness you use as you listen to someone else. Neither you nor the other person has to use a particular formula in speaking.

In the pages that follow, I'll review the essence of Rosenberg's enormously helpful system.[4]

OBSERVING VERSUS EVALUATING

Learn to separate your observations from your evaluations. Simply observe what you are seeing, feeling, touching, and hearing (and sometimes smelling or tasting), and realize that your observation is distinct from your conclusion, opinion, belief, or judgment.

Another piece of this important distinction is being clear with others that something is your own evaluation or opinion ("I thought the play was really dull") rather than stating your opinion as if it were a fact ("That play sucked").

To get a taste of this, compare both parts of each of these sets of statements:

- He's a jerk. (Evaluation with no observation.)
- He made three sexual comments about women who walked by. (Observation.) That creeps me out. (Evaluation.)

- Her mom is great. (Evaluation with no observation.)
- Her mom took us to the art museum. She seems generous to me. (Observation first, evaluation second.)

- Edna is a whiner. (The term *whiner* mixes an observation with an evaluation.)

- Edna and I rode the bus to town and she talked nonstop about being unhappy with everyone in her life. (Observation.) I don't want to spend my time that way. (Evaluation.)

- You're pushy. (Evaluation with no observation.)
- You raised your voice just now. I don't like that. (Observation first, evaluation second.)

- You just can't think straight, can you? (Evaluation and accusation.)
- You changed the subject twice in the last five minutes. I'm thinking you're trying to avoid talking about this. (Observation first, evaluation second.)

IDENTIFYING AND EXPRESSING YOUR FEELINGS

Expressing your feelings, either to yourself or to others, brings you personally into the picture, especially when you follow a statement of observation with a statement of your feeling about it. Identifying and expressing your feelings requires that you look into yourself, notice your feelings, and say what those feelings are.

Here are some examples:

- He made three sexual comments about women who walked by. That creeps me out. I felt more vulnerable and uneasy with each comment.
- Her mom took us to the art museum. She seems generous to me. I enjoyed myself.
- Edna and I rode the bus to town and she talked nonstop about being unhappy with everyone in her life. I was bored and cross by the time we got there.
- You raised your voice just now. I don't like that. I got scared.
- You changed the subject twice in the last five minutes. I'm thinking you're trying to avoid talking about this. I'm irritated.

Feeling versus Thinking

Sometimes people say they are feeling something when what they are expressing is really a thought. In the following pairs of statements, which is a feeling?

1a. I feel crushed.
1b. I feel that you are selfish.

2a. I feel Mary is clever.
2b. I'm delighted by your comments.

3a. I love you.
3b. I feel that I love you.

Inserting the word *that* changes the statement to a thought, even if a feeling word is used. Also using the word *feel* does not guarantee that a feeling will follow. Most feelings don't need the word *feel*.

Answers: 1a, 2b, and 3a are expressing feelings. The other statements are actually thoughts.

TAKING RESPONSIBILITY FOR FEELINGS AND EXPRESSING THE NEEDS BEHIND THEM

We may be hurt by something someone else does or says, but no one forces us to feel. Our feelings arise from inside us as a result of our unique mix of issues, history, vulnerability, awareness, and needs. Our personal degree of vulnerability varies according to our mindfulness, centeredness, tiredness, and stress level, much of which we can make choices about.

Listen to—and feel—the difference between these two statements:

- You hurt me.
- I was hurt when you canceled our anniversary date because honoring our time together matters to me.

We often think the reason for a feeling is obvious. And if the second statement had included only the feeling half of the sentence—"I was hurt when you canceled our anniversary date"—we might say, "Of course he's hurt. Anybody would be."

That may be true, but Ed could be hurt because he'd been looking forward to time with Edna without the kids, while Paul might be hurt because he was planning to wow Paula with a brass band and a skywriter, and now his plans and money are down the drain.

Revealing the thoughts or hopes behind a feeling conveys more meaning, and that lets both you and the other person know more about you.

Behind most feelings are needs. Paying attention to what you need and expressing that need is your best chance at getting it fulfilled.

- I was hurt when you canceled our anniversary date because honoring our time together matters to me. At certain times I need to feel regrounded in our marriage, and for me that means putting our union first now and then.
- He made three sexual comments about women who walked by. That creeps me out. I felt more vulnerable and uneasy with each comment. I want to feel safe when I am with a man.
- Her mom took us to the art museum. She seems generous to me. I enjoyed myself. I didn't even know how much I needed a day of Renoir wallowing until we got there.
- Edna and I rode the bus to town and she talked nonstop about being unhappy with everyone in her life. I was bored and cross by the time we got there. I want to be with people who look at things positively most of the time. I'm trying to learn to notice the good in life. I'm already skilled at noticing what's wrong.
- You raised your voice just now. I don't like that. I got scared. I need to feel safe when we disagree.
- You changed the subject twice in the last five minutes. I'm thinking you're trying to avoid talking about this. I'm irritated. I would like to say all of my thoughts about this issue so I can figure out what my point is.

ASKING FOR THINGS THAT ENRICH LIFE

One of the best communication tools is a clear, straightforward request. Here are some helpful guidelines:

1. Ask for what you want or need in a way that invites a clear, direct response.
2. Express what you want instead of what you don't want.
3. Ask for specific, concrete things and actions.
4. If you have doubts about whether your message was correctly received, ask your listener to restate the content of your message back to you.
5. If you want to know what your listener is feeling or thinking in response to your message, ask her to tell you.
6. If your listener doesn't give you a clear, unambiguous answer, ask if he will grant your request.

Here are some examples of these principles:

- I was hurt when you canceled our anniversary date because honoring our time together matters to me. At certain times I need to feel regrounded in our marriage, and for me that means putting our union first now and then. Would you arrange a date for us next Friday and make the reservations and get a baby-sitter?
- Her mom took us to the art museum. She seems generous to me. I enjoyed myself. I didn't even know how much I needed a day of Renoir wallowing until we got there. I want to go to the Burke museum in two weeks. Would you be willing to go with me?
- You raised your voice just now. I don't like that. I got scared. I need to feel safe when we disagree. Does it bother you that I have a different opinion on the subject? And I do want you to talk to me about it, but not when you raise your voice. Are you willing to keep your tone in the talking range while we discuss it?
- You changed the subject twice in the last five minutes.

I'm thinking that you're trying to avoid talking about this. I'm irritated. I would like to say all of my thoughts about this issue so that I can figure out what my point is. I want you to listen quietly to me without saying anything for the next five minutes. Are you willing?

LISTENING WITH EMPATHY

When you listen to others, offer them the same compassion and attention that you'd like from them. Here are Rosenberg's components of compassionate responding:

- being fully present
- listening for feelings and needs
- paraphrasing
- feeling and sustaining empathy[5]

USING COMPASSIONATE COMMUNICATION
WITH YOURSELF

Although Rosenberg's system is intended for use in relationships with others, it also works splendidly in your communication with yourself.

Misery addicts are often divided inside. Faction one is determined to protect the self from being hurt. Faction two wants to experience more good in life.

The protective part, faction one, usually feels very young. This is because at a tender and vulnerable age you had to come up with a way to survive. You developed principles to minimize the harm that was done to you, and these led to strategies and decisions that are still operating today. Faction one has amazing strength and at times is more powerful than your own adult mind (faction two).

One way to connect your two factions is to use these same techniques of communication: observe an action, express your feeling about it, explain the need, and make a clear request. Then the other side listens, paraphrases, and responds.

I encourage you to try talking faction to faction out loud so that the process is clear and memorable. It can also be exceedingly enlightening to set up two chairs, one for each faction, and to switch chairs as each faction speaks. (Don't do this in public, of course, or in front of anyone who won't understand and appreciate what you're doing. Although the process is very valuable—and very sane—to someone familiar with it, it may look either crazy or like some Acting 101 assignment to the uninitiated.)

Here are some examples of the process:

Anne 1: I noticed that when you started writing Monday, you didn't meditate beforehand. I felt vexed because I like the writing to go smoothly, and when you meditate, it does. I feel like blaming you, but I won't because it won't help. But feeling deeper into myself, I know I feel angry. I need to be able to count on you to follow through with what works for us. Are you willing to listen and respond by meditating when your spiritual source beckons?

Anne 2: I'm taking in your need to stay spiritually connected when you write. I agree that the writing always goes better when you do that. But I remember that on Monday I woke up so excited about writing that I just wanted to start as soon as possible. When I feel deeper into myself, I see that at times I feel rebellious and want to do it by myself. Now that I've looked at this, I understand myself better. I feel willing to be responsive when I hear my spiritual source calling me.

Anne 1: Thank you for listening and honoring my request.

Kali Rose: Little Kali Rose, when you went to therapy Tuesday and sat there without speaking, I felt so frustrated. I need something to happen in therapy, and it doesn't when you won't talk. I need to use therapy to move me forward, and I want my money to go to good use too. I want you to talk next week. If you have to write out what you want to say before we get there and read it, then I want you to do that.

Little Kali Rose: Kali Rose, I want to talk too. But when I sit there, I get paralyzed. I want the therapist's attention, but I'm mad too, because she just keeps being my therapist and I want her to be my mom. Every time she leaves or I leave, I feel like I did when I was little and Mom left. Then I get so mad at her I want to spit.

Kali Rose: Little Kali Rose, I can hear that you feel divided. One part pushes while the other part pulls. I understand that. It really hurt us when Mom left. It sounds to me like you're afraid that if you get too close to the therapist, it'll hurt more if something happens to her. Yet when we trust her, we feel better inside and more connected.

Little Kali Rose: I'm willing to write out what I want to talk about beforehand, and I agree to read it if I feel stuck.

Kali Rose: I think it would help to talk about being paralyzed, too, and about the different impulses that clash for us when that happens.

Little Kali Rose: Maybe that's what I should write about first.

Kali Rose: Great idea.

KEEPING A GRATITUDE JOURNAL

It sounds so simple. It's easy to dismiss the power of gratitude. But the truth is that gratitude is incredibly powerful.

Most days, for most people, something goes right. A misery addict can easily miss it though, especially if she's feeling grouchy, depressed, or frightened—and if she's looking for (or expecting) things to go wrong.

This is why it's a good daily practice to keep a simple gratitude journal. At the end of each day, just take five minutes to list five things you are grateful for. That's it. Do this for one month and observe what happens.

Keeping a gratitude journal removes our dark glasses. At first we may have to look hard to find something to put in it, but over

time it gets easier, and we feel more and more positive about ourselves and our life.

FORGIVING

Many in recovery, especially women, have been physically or sexually abused, and some have been pressured by religious figures or
traditions to forgive their abusers. But there's a potential problem
here.

When we think of forgiveness as letting the abuser off easy or
saying it was okay to cause us harm, we only damage ourselves further. Premature forgiveness cuts off our essential feelings of anger.

Consultant and speaker Constance Wolfe, M.S.W., teaches that
there is a difference between spiritual forgiveness and psychological forgiveness.[6] Psychological forgiveness happens when we've
processed our pain as deeply as necessary and we are able to let go
of the person who harmed us. We have to wait to do this kind of
forgiving until it's a natural outgrowth of our recovery process.

Spiritual forgiveness is different—it's a spiritual release of the
other person. This we can do at any point. For example, we can
think, *I forgive you from my spiritual nature. I forgive you spiritually, knowing that your highest self would not have chosen to
harm me.*

But we don't use spiritual forgiveness to tell ourselves that we
didn't get hurt. We continue to know the truth about what happened to us.

Spiritual forgiveness allows us to release our resentment.

TOOL BELT

For emergencies, fasten on this tool belt. If something happens that
upsets you or threatens your recovery, use one of the following
tools.

Make the MOST of your day:

> **M**ake Hay/Mine for Gold
> **O**pposite Action
> **S**teps
> **T**alk

Make Hay or Mine for Gold

If a feeling upsets you, take advantage of it. Use the Healthy Feeling Process from chapter 26 to find out about yourself. Make hay while the feeling strikes. Mine for the meaning. It could be a new twist on an old issue or just a warning shot that you need to take better care of yourself. Pay attention to it and let it inform you.

Opposite Action

Do the opposite thing from what you traditionally do to avoid or hide from the situation. If you usually get silent, deliberately speak. If you usually run away, stay. If you let others go first, you go first. If you sacrifice, ask for what you want. If you push yourself, rest. If you isolate yourself, call a friend.

Steps One, Two, Three

Say the first three Steps of the Twelve Steps, out loud if possible. Or use the quickie version: "I can't. God can. I'll let Her."

Talk

Call a recovering friend or your sponsor, and tell him what's happening to you and how you feel. For a cherry on top, ask for comforting words and a virtual hug.

CHAPTER TWENTY-EIGHT

Brain Healing

Does trauma cause brain damage? Yes. Can the brain heal? Yes.

Trauma alters the very platelets in our bloodstream. It affects the configuration of neurons in the brain, the quantity and proportion of neurotransmitters, and the development or shrinkage of brain matter.

Fortunately, we can do things that reverse the damage done to the brain. Unfortunately, we can't undo the configuration of addiction. Those branches in the brain are permanent—which is why, if you reexpose yourself to your addiction, it settles right back in as though it never had a vacation. Any addict can tell you that it's difficult to work against your own brain.

However, you can get your brain on your side. Through conscious practices, you can bring new growth to the brain that makes it easier, over time, to consistently make healthy choices. As your brain heals, the brain itself will help you stay on the healthier path.

BRAIN FOOD

You need to feed your brain well. This may seem really obvious. Yet people inside an addiction will not consider inadequate nutrition as something that contributes to their distorted thinking.

An addiction distorts thinking because of direct chemical action on the brain. However, thinking also gets distorted because of what you *aren't* eating as a result of the addiction's influence on your appetite or food preferences.

If you had a sick baby, you would want to be very careful about his nutrition and his exposure to harmful influences. While your own brain is healing, you need to be just as careful.

Here are some tips on how to feed your brain well:

- Your brain needs about two hundred calories every couple of hours when it is healing.[1] Every two hours (except, of course, while you're asleep), give yourself some protein.
- If you are a sugar addict, highly sweet foods will throw off your brain chemistry. Eat whole fruits, not juices or dried fruit. Use stevia (a natural sweetener made from the leaves of the stevia plant) to sweeten drinks, cereal, or desserts. Most food co-ops, health food stores, and many supermarkets carry stevia. (Stevia is thought to balance blood sugar.)
- Drink about a glass of water every ninety minutes (more in hot or arid environments or when sweating or losing fluids). Your brain is 85 percent water. Getting dehydrated can make you cranky and distort your thinking.
- Eat high-quality whole grains such as oatmeal or brown rice to promote clear thinking.
- Broccoli, cabbage, salads, and raw vegetables provide phytochemicals that the brain needs for neurotransmission and healing.
- Nuts, cheese, fish, and eggs are sometimes called "smart foods" because they increase the amount of choline in the brain, which enhances memory and attention.
- Certain minerals and vitamins, such as magnesium, omega-3 fatty acids, and vitamins C and E promote brain healing and repair. For dosage and to check interactions with other medications, consult a medical professional or a book on nutritional healing. A fine source is Dr. Russell Blaylock's book *Excitotoxins*.

A person on psychotropic medications (such as antidepressants) will suffer more from side effects if she is low in protein. Anorexics, people malnourished from addiction, and binge eaters who have neglected their protein intake are at more risk for these side effects. The answer: eat more protein.

Being thoughtful about feeding your brain helps your thinking improve.

FOODS THAT CAN HURT YOU

Certain common foods can harm you and your recovery. Dr. Blaylock blew the whistle on a major category of such foods with his book *Excitotoxins*.

Aspartame (the important ingredient in NutraSweet), hydrolyzed vegetable protein, and monosodium glutamate (MSG) are excitotoxins, which are being associated more and more with degenerative brain diseases, brain cell death, nervous system disorders, strokes, brain damage, seizures, hypoglycemic brain damage, and migraine headaches.[2]

Food manufacturers like MSG because it can make ordinary food taste scrumptious, removes the tinny flavor of canned foods, and suppresses undesirable flavors. Since the late 1940s, the amount of MSG added to prepared foods has doubled every decade.[3]

MSG is disguised with innocent sounding labels like vegetable protein, hydrolyzed vegetable protein, and natural flavorings. Hydrolyzed vegetable protein and MSG are added to many foods, including beef broth, chips, frozen foods, fast foods, and toddler foods. Blaylock's book states, "The amount of MSG in a single bowl of commercially available soup is probably enough to cause blood glutamate levels to rise higher in a human child than levels that predictably cause brain damage in immature animals."[4]

Glutamate is a naturally occurring brain amino acid. The problem comes from flooding the brain with unnatural amounts of that chemical beyond the brain's capacity to siphon it out or in areas unprotected by the brain's natural barrier, such as the hypothalamus and locus coeruleus[5] (areas already implicated in several addictions). Excessive amounts of glutamate can cause serious problems including nerve cell destruction. In animals MSG caused destruction of hypothalamic cells causing obesity, reproductive problems, and early onset of puberty.[6]

If you value your brain, stop eating any food containing MSG, aspartame (NutraSweet), or hydrolyzed vegetable protein.

CLEARING

Research shows that psychotherapy helps the brain. This is not exactly a big surprise to those of us in the business.

The very best timing for psychotherapy is immediately following trauma. We've seen this in action in recent years when communities or schools are flooded with crisis counselors following a tragedy.

Immediate therapy prevents trauma from settling into the tissues of the body, especially the brain. (We therapists call this process consolidation.) Consolidation can start within a week after the trauma and can continue for more than twenty years past the event.

Of course, starting therapy at any time, even years or decades after trauma, is better than continued waiting.

The most important component of therapy is talking out the experience with immediacy and presence. Immediacy means that as you talk, it's as if you were there. The present surroundings fade, and you see the event in your mind's eye. Presence means you are present to the experience, fully inside it, instead of talking about it as if it happened to somebody else.

The second most important component of therapy is the quality of the therapist's listening. Nonjudgmental, empathic, receptive listening is more important—and does much more good—than advice, pep talks, or commands to buck up, which only cut off internal processing and healing.

EXERCISE

Mild exercise improves protein balance in the body by increasing muscle tone. Exercise also increases blood flow and oxygen intake and lifts your mood.

Twenty percent of blood flow and 20 percent of oxygen intake go into the brain. When you improve circulation and oxygen intake, the brain gets a big benefit. So does the rest of your body.

SLEEP

An injured body part needs rest. The brain is no exception. It needs plenty of downtime to get itself in order.

Between the hours of 9 P.M. and midnight, most people's brains manufacture body-healing hormones. Stress and excessive late-day activity can interfere with the body's appointment to heal itself.

Because your brain is healing, stop doing anything that pressures you after 9 P.M. Be in bed by 10:00 as much as possible.

You can help yourself sleep with a daily dose of serotonin by eating a few ounces of turkey each day or drinking a cup of warm milk before bedtime.

REPROGRAMMING

The brain is the body's computer, and it is susceptible to reprogramming. You can counteract a childhood of negative messages by giving your brain positive messages. Affirmations, visualization, and preenactment are all ways to soak your mind in new thought.

An *affirmation* is a positive "I" statement in the present tense:

My life improves daily.
I make good decisions for myself.
I attract positive people who offer good to me.
I see opportunities.
I act quickly and positively when good is offered.

Visualization is mentally picturing the good you want. The classic reference on this subject is Shakti Gawain's book *Creative Visualization*. You can use your imagination, drawing, collage, or clay to create a detailed picture of the way you want your life to be. Picture the kind of people you want in it. Feel how you want to feel. See yourself doing what you want to do.

Preenactment is acting out your visualization with your body. If you want to be good at fishing, imitate the actions of fishing with a smile on your face and positive energy in your heart. Become increasingly precise with your enactment, adding as many details as you can think of that involve that activity.

Many of us have discovered the effectiveness of a spiritual principle called *attraction*. We have found that we can attract good into our lives by using the three practices just described, along with prayer and meditation.

BRAIN EXERCISE

Like the body, the brain likes to be exercised. A bored brain turns off part of itself. Learning, new experiences, puzzles, reading, and sensory exposure (such as concerts and art museums) give the brain something to do.

Childhood trauma can isolate the brain halves. A major highway connecting the right and left hemispheres is called the corpus callosum. Trauma can decrease commerce between these two.

Drawing on the Right Side of the Brain by Betty Edwards is specifically aimed at healing this bridge. Although one's drawing skills improve through the exercises in her book, the main benefit is strengthened access to the right brain and improved transmission between the brain halves.

Another good book, *Keep Your Brain Alive* by Lawrence Katz et al. offers other exercises to give your brain a workout.

Go home a different way, learn a new language, stop to smell the lilacs, study the different patterns on the wings of finches, do puzzles, sing, watch bubbles; all sorts of simple activities open the windows of the mind.

MEDICATION

The medications available at present, such as antidepressants or antipsychotics, do not, so far as I know, heal the brain. They do, however, bring the brain up to speed, allowing it to function close to a normal range. The advantage of this in terms of healing is that a malfunctioning part puts strain on the other healthy parts.

A brain that is underutilizing serotonin receptors, for example, is a brain too agitated and not getting enough rest, which would seem to overuse other neurons and use up other neurotransmitters.

We do our brains a service, if we need medication, to take the appropriate kind and dose.

ALLOW THE BENEFIT TO CONSOLIDATE

Here's a very important principle: after you've taken yourself through a Healthy Feeling Process (see chapter 26) and have experienced a shift or insight, or after you've received enough comfort to be able to let an issue go, stay on the new side of the divide you've crossed.

We can feel so good about a discovery or new feeling of liberation that we want to tell people how we got there. So we cross back over the bridge and rehash the details of the event that upset us, providing the background so our listener can appreciate the grandeur of our new vantage.

CAUTION: By reawakening those feelings, you can pull yourself back to your old place of misery. You can even lose your revelation.

I remember the first time I was flooded with revelation. I thought, *I'll never forget this. This is the most incredible discovery of my life.* It was like a golden door had opened on a distant vista. And then, in trying to describe the entire process to somebody, I lost it and couldn't get it back.

So stay in your joy. Rest in your revelation. Write it down so that you can remember the details. Talk about the shift all you like, but avoid going back over the ground that brought you there.

Remember the information about trauma settling into body tissues if it is not processed? This is the opposite situation. You *want* this to settle in. You want the revelation, the rise in energy, the joy to settle into your body. You want it to be recorded.

So keep yourself on the positive side. Once you've crossed over, don't go back over the old divide for at least a month. If you start to talk about the old place and you feel a dip in energy or rising dread, quit talking about it. Switch immediately to talking about the joy and the discovery.

This next piece of advice is crucial: do not tell joyous discoveries to people who have hurt you. Protect your tender tendrils.

Reveal your discoveries only to those who can celebrate with you. If you start to share joyous information with someone who begins messing with it, stop. That person will try to turn it against you and put you right back into your old misery. Don't allow that. Preserve your joy.

CHAPTER TWENTY-NINE

Therapy

Therapy and recovery combined are a dynamic duo. Recovery gives you a conscious mind and a process that renovates your life. Therapy gets to the root of the issues that first turned you toward addiction.

In the twenty-first century, many types of therapy are available, ranging from left-brained, logical, rational therapies to flowing, process-oriented, experiential therapies. The injuries that lead to misery addiction are generally more responsive to process-centered therapies, such as depth therapy or certain talk therapies in which the relationship with the therapist is the healing tool.

However, do look for a therapist who also knows about addiction. A therapist not wise about the subject can be fooled by your misery addiction. Your therapist also needs to know the importance of the recovery process and be able to see the signs of relapse.

You especially need a therapist who understands that addiction cannot be controlled. Therapies that are based on control (and there are some that have proven effective for some people, though not for people with addictions) will just set you up by feeding the fantasy that enough control can make your misery addiction go away. You've already wasted huge chunks of time chasing this impossible goal.

This therapy should be about you. You need a process designed to assist you in discovering yourself and in helping you visit your own depths, within which are the tender histories that have shaped your life.

Look for a therapist you feel good with, someone who can really see you for who you are, someone you click with and feel safe with.

Choose someone who is honest and who knows how to be present.

Choose a professional who loves her work because she will operate out of passion more than out of a profit motive. She will also give her work an extra measure of involvement.

Since misery addiction is a relatively new concept, I've included a letter to therapists (see appendix B). This letter refers therapists to my Web site for additional information. A good therapist will be willing to read this material and use the guidelines in it to help you.

All therapists make mistakes. No one is perfect. Sooner or later yours will do something that makes you angry. Sometimes it's a true mistake, in which case you get to explore how you feel when someone you trust screws up. Sometimes it's a projected mistake—one that you only imagined. In this case, because of your perspective, your issues, or your actions, you see your therapist in a light that reflects you more than him. It is your therapist's job to help you discover something about yourself that is revealed by that projection.

A therapist's mistake (real or perceived) is always fertile therapeutic ground—not a good reason to quit therapy. You can let that be your excuse if you want, but you'll get more out of talking about it with your therapist and learning from it.

You probably already know that anyone in a position of authority for you should not be sexual with you. If this happens, find a new therapist immediately.

A good therapist is like a good parent. She notices you, pays attention to you, reflects you, counsels you, listens to you, is on your side, shows you to yourself, and offers genuine affection.

A therapist is not, however, charged with doing more for you than you are willing to do for yourself. Although your therapist has experience dealing with resistance, if you dig your heels in and fight him at every turn, he is not required to be more powerful than your "no." He can witness it, he can offer options, and he can care about you stuck inside it, but he is not required to engage in conflict with you. You are sovereign over your life, your body, and your therapy. You can sabotage it, or you can decide to let it work.

Some therapists supplement their traditional skills with other approaches that enhance the therapy experience. Some of these are energy work, nutrition counseling, Reiki (energy healing), hypnotherapy, past-life therapy, toning, body work, color therapy, light therapy, rebirthing, reparenting, spiritual enhancement, and group work. In the case of therapy, more is usually better. Of course, the better the therapist, the more valuable the therapy.

Since misery addicts tend to give themselves less than what they need, therapy is a good place for opposite action. Give yourself more than just the basic experience. If your therapist leads retreats, go to one. If she has another skill, try it. Approach therapy with an openness for change.

It can be a typical self-sabotaging decision to limit your therapy sessions to whatever your insurance coverage provides. The badly designed lottery called mental health insurance rarely covers the number of sessions a person actually needs to reach all but the simplest therapeutic goals. Plus, while many good therapists are approved for insurance coverage, many other good ones are not. Few people at any insurance company actually know the covered therapists or anything about the quality of their work. Therefore, don't limit your search for a good therapist to the list in your health insurance book, especially if your insurance covers only a paltry number of sessions.

You need a therapist who understands and can foster a healthy attachment, who understands what is meant by a secure base and safe haven, and who knows how to support a person in recovery. If he has an understanding of misery addiction, even better.

This is the quality of the rest of your life we're talking about here. Getting the right kind of help will pay you back tenfold. It will rescue your remaining days on earth and help you to, at long last, live and enjoy some of your dreams.

CHAPTER THIRTY

Making It Last

or

Avoiding Relapse

Relapse is the precipitous or gradual slide back into the self-destructive practices and attitudes of addiction. Relapse is usually triggered. The trigger is usually some event that causes a sudden internal fall off of the scaffolding erected by recovery.

The following examples could be experienced as a result of a dire event that has actually happened:

- a severe disappointment
- a threat to your survival
- something that interrupts your feeling of safety
- the loss of your home base
- feeling shame or being shamed

However, such experiences could also be spawned by our own thoughts in reaction to a misperception, a projection, or being triggered into an old, buried hurt or shame.

For example, we could shame ourselves with a thought, or someone could say something shaming. A chance remark by a boss could feel like a severe threat to survival, triggering a flare of relapse as our own fear flames but not denote anything serious from his point of view.

Time and again, the initiating event is quickly forgotten as the slide toward relapse commences. Suddenly, your consciousness shifts from having a recovery orientation to having a comfort-seeking orientation. This shift in orientation causes a shift in behaviors, such as skipping a meeting, putting yourself in a slippery place, or exposing yourself to a tool addiction.

These secondary events then set up the environment of use, whether one's use will be a substance like sugar or alcohol or a return to an activity addiction like computer game-playing or caretaking.

Later, when we autopsy a relapse, we may identify the secondary event as the causal event, saying something such as, "I shouldn't have gone into that bakery," as if the bakery were the stimulus. But a misery addict with sugar as one of the tool addictions knows full well that a bakery is a slippery place with the inevitable outcome of eating a sugar product because of the overpowering stimulation of its sights and smells.

The question really is, "Why in the world did I go into a bakery? I had to know before I stepped through the door that I was setting myself up with nearly a 100 percent chance of succumbing to a product."

We find the answer by working our way back to the shift in consciousness. What happened before the bakery? What happened before that? We keep going back until we can approach the question: what was it that caused my shift from recovery consciousness to addictive consciousness?

Relapse can be caused, also, by exposure to the addictive substance or activity, by hanging out with people who use your substance or promote your activity, or by frequenting places that push the substance or activity.

You become more vulnerable to relapse whenever you let your recovery support activities lapse. Missing meetings, not talking to a partner in recovery, not talking about your issues at meetings or therapy group, skipping therapy—in short, any way you decrease your contact with other people who carry recovery consciousness—

is a setup for eventual relapse. It's like taking down the safety net and storing it in the basement. The next time you get knocked off the tightrope, you'll have a hard fall instead of bouncing back. Lapse leads to relapse.

What's going on in our insides when we let ourselves lapse? Here are some of the possibilities:

- a stubborn feeling, "I can do it myself."
- feeling defiant, "I don't need you to tell me how to run my life."
- shame, "I don't deserve it."
- onset of denial, "I'm doing so well, I don't need meetings anymore."
- the creep of unmanageability, "I'm too busy."

All of the above are aspects of forgetting the truth—that we are powerless over our addictions and compulsions and we need other people in order to stay in right relationship with ourselves and others.

RELAPSE IS THE OPPOSITE OF RECOVERY

Anyone with an addiction is vulnerable to relapse. It's not inevitable, but lots of people in all recovery programs relapse. It's really quite normal. If you relapse and start blaming or shaming yourself, that's actually a part of the relapse.

Remember that a relapse can be prevented or stopped by noticing when you are starting to let your recovery efforts slide or when you are starting to have an attitude of defiance, stubbornness, shame, or hopelessness.

Three telltale signs for a misery addict are an increase in avoidance, self-sabotage, or interest in tool addictions. During their first year or two of recovery, most misery addicts are susceptible to reverting to their old patterns if they don't maintain conscious efforts toward recovery. For your own progress to last, you need to keep yourself connected to a recovery community.

The minute you notice an increase in self-sabotage, run, don't walk, to your community (and your sponsor, if you have one) and increase your contact there. You can lose your gains so quickly that your head will spin. Don't risk it. Don't risk having to start over. Fix it fast because the deeper you let yourself sink, the more likely it is you will have to start at the beginning to get yourself out of the pit again.

Following are two common characteristics of addiction:

1. Addiction is progressive. Over time an addiction will always get worse.
2. If you relapse and pick up your addiction again—whether two months or twenty years later—the addiction has progressed, and you will practice it beyond your level of use before you stopped.

I saw this so graphically when I quit smoking many years ago. I cherished the fantasy held by all addicts that since I had quit, I could now have a cigarette occasionally without falling back into addiction. So I accepted a cigarette. By the next day I was smoking more than before I had quit. (I am grateful to say that I've now been abstinent from tobacco for twenty-two years.)

The changes in the brain that come from addiction don't go away. They stay in place. As a result, whenever the addictive practice is reintroduced to the body, the brain already has the mechanism to welcome it and proceed from there.

Once you let yourself flirt with your addiction again, the slide into relapse will be swift. The next thing that will happen is that some aspect of your self-care or recovery slips. *That slip is your visible sign that something has happened.* This is the point when you need to get to your community or call a recovering friend fast.

Without action *at this exact point,* you will be back in your addiction tomorrow.

YOUR SAFETY NET

Once you have lapsed or relapsed, your next most important action is to get back with your recovery community and increase your recovery contacts. Sometimes we feel ashamed for having relapsed, and we feel reluctant to tell other program people, thinking it makes us look like failures. We are not perfect, and no person in true recovery will judge us. We all know how powerful and cunning addiction is and that it is grace and benevolence that has saved each one of us.

Still, your recovery activities are your safety net. If you are meticulous about keeping that process active, then when a dangerous feeling or event comes along, you already have the structure in place to catch you and keep you from falling.

CHAPTER THIRTY-ONE

Is It Really an Addiction?

Should misery addiction properly be called an addiction? You bet.

There are three easy tests to see if something is an addiction. Here's the oldest.

TEST 1

If you remove the substance or activity, does the person experience withdrawal? Do the symptoms of withdrawal disappear when the substance or activity is reintroduced? Then when you remove it a second time, does withdrawal reoccur?

Symptoms of withdrawal—disorientation, mood swings, sudden bursts of anger or rage, a change in sleeping patterns, a change in appetite—are all indicative of the brain having a fit, of neurons missing chemicals they are used to receiving. Withdrawal occurs in a predictable pattern for a predictable number of days, depending on the substance or activities involved.

Do misery addicts experience withdrawal? Hoo boy! Here at our retreat center we call it Hell Week.

Remember, one characteristic of misery addiction is using a constellation of tool addictions that, while temporarily soothing the misery, actually increase it. When a misery addict is separated from all of her addictions and is unable to sabotage herself, it isn't pretty.

What makes a misery addict feel better? Let him be on his own for a weekend, making all of his own decisions. He'll get right back into his comfortable groove of sabotaging himself—and all the withdrawal will go away.

TEST 2

Something is an addiction if

- a person experiences strong, irresistible cravings for the substance or activity.
- the person continues to use the substance or persist in the activity despite predictable negative consequences.
- due to that activity or substance, the person experiences a series of increasingly serious losses.

Misery addiction passes this test with flying colors. Self-sabotaging actions can be many and varied. Whatever set of these behaviors a misery addict uses, the need for them is so great that she can't stop herself from doing them. Even in the midst of a very pleasant, healthy activity, a craving for the familiar self-sabotage will begin to intrude on her experience.

A misery addict suffers losses in his health, relationships, finances, time, and career. Yet despite knowing that self-sabotaging actions will mess up things, he keeps doing them.

TEST 3

There is one other way to identify addiction: does recovery fix it? Do the methods that emancipate alcoholics, drug addicts, gamblers, and food addicts work for misery addicts too?

Yes, indeed. Misery addiction responds well to the principles and practices of traditional recovery programs. The same type of recovery program that rescues the lives of other addicts rescues misery addicts as well.

The corollary to the above question is: does therapy alone *not* fix it?

For most addictions, even the best therapy doesn't separate the user from her drug. A food addict will still seek sugar and a smoker will still smoke. Excellent therapy can heal the influence of the past, but it doesn't fix the physiological alterations the body has made due to the addiction.

Misery addiction also passes this test. Therapy alone does not reverse it.

Misery addiction is an addiction to avoidance, to self-sabotage, and to a system of survival that results in a loss of joy, intimacy, and potential. *Recovery is also a system.* The recovery process gives the misery addict a new, different, and healthier system to substitute for the old one.

THE PHYSIOLOGY OF ADDICTION

In recent years, the technology for studying the human brain has advanced remarkably, yielding information previously only dreamed of.

Each year we come closer to identifying the specific mechanisms of addiction. For the traditional addictions—alcohol, drugs, sugar, and so on—we are discovering ever more about the neurotransmitters involved and the specific physical locations triggered within the brain. Research into activity addictions such as gambling, sex addiction, workaholism, and caretaking is not as advanced, but I believe strongly that soon we will be able to pinpoint how these mechanisms work in the brain as well.

Lastly, we are now beginning to identify physical correlates of trauma, often a precondition for addiction. Remember, most misery addicts are trauma survivors.

CHAPTER THIRTY-TWO

Make a Commitment to Yourself

If you've read most of the chapters in this book, then deep in your heart you want to leave the valley of misery.

And you can. You were not destined to stay there.

You'll need to help yourself remember to actively do things that keep you from sliding back into misery. Remember that you are vulnerable to sabotaging yourself. Write a sticky note, set an alarm in your computer or Palm Pilot, or do something else that will remind you from time to time to take positive action. Here are some slogans you can use.

> I am powerless, but my Higher Power is not.
> I'll let my Higher Power guide me.
> Remember my Daily Practice.
> Make the MOST of my feelings.
> Come into this moment.
> Joy is good for me.
> What am I grateful for?
> I will stay committed to my life.

Recovering misery addicts are susceptible to three self-sabotaging choices:

1. reducing or eliminating their contact with their recovery community.
2. spending time with people who criticize them, use them, or hurt them.
3. abandoning their commitment to themselves.

Stay committed to yourself and your life. When something goes wrong or someone says something hurtful, you are vulnerable to thoughts such as *What's the use?* or *I might as well give up.*

Don't succumb to these. Things do go wrong from time to time for everyone; that's why there's a bumper sticker about it.

REVERSE

- Don't get stuck in reverse magical thinking, in your old beliefs that things can't work out for you. Remember, you learned such beliefs because of how you were treated.
- Don't let yourself be treated badly by anyone, not even yourself. Tell the person to stop, or just leave.
- Remember that, most of the time, when things don't work out, it's due to one of these causes: (1) a failure to plan and follow through; (2) not listening to your instincts; (3) risking too much with hurtful or thoughtless people; or (4) not risking enough with healthy, loving people.
- Don't spend time with people who can trigger a slide back into misery. You lose options once you are triggered. I repeat: you have much more choice *before* you are triggered. The best thing you can do with people who will treat you poorly is to stay away from them. Sometimes this may mean staying away from members of your own family.

Often, when we've been victimized as children, we tend to drift into a victimized stance as adults. One way we play this out is by waiting passively for someone else to do whatever will make something work.

Stop waiting. It's your life. So go ahead; you make it work out. You have the power. Don't depend on someone else who may have a different agenda.

ADVANCE!

- Make a commitment to yourself. Keep this commitment.
- Take active steps to get what you want for yourself. Ask for things. Ask for opportunities.
- Stay conscious and in the moment. Stay thoughtful.
- Ask for and use help. Don't turn down good help when it is offered.
- Spend plenty of time with other people in recovery.
- Keep your mind alert by staying abstinent from mind-dulling substances and activities.
- If you feel overwhelmed, ride out the wave. The word *over-whelm* comes from seafaring Scandinavia and refers to water washing over the helm of the ship. When water rushes over your helm, put on a life preserver and start paddling.
- If something goes wrong, review it to see if you set up a negative outcome. Learn from it. Figure out how you can make better choices for yourself next time.
- Take responsibility for yourself and the quality of your life.

You can rise into joy. It is possible. Truly.

ACCEPT YOUR SPIRITUAL CALLING TO BE JOYFUL

You were born into circumstances that you were meant to move beyond.

Your spiritual sources do not want you to suffer. They want you to accept the challenge of climbing to joy. It is your destiny and your purpose.

You are unique. Your life is required. Live fully into the promise of your life—now.

APPENDIXES

APPENDIX A

*MAA Meeting Information**

Feel free to copy anything in this appendix. No permission is needed.

MEETING GUIDE

Most MAA (Misery Addicts Anonymous/Multiple Addictions Anonymous) meetings last sixty or ninety minutes and meet once a week.

Starting the Meeting

Following is an opening dialogue for an MAA meeting. Start on time, even if you are the only one there.

> Good Morning. Welcome to the _____ meeting of the _____ group of Misery Addicts Anonymous. My name is _____.
> I am a misery addict, and I am the chairperson for today. This is an open meeting, and we are glad that you are here, especially newcomers.
> Please join me in a moment of silence to reflect on the reasons we are here, followed by the Serenity Prayer.
>
> God, grant me the serenity
> to accept the things I cannot change,
> courage to change the things I can,
> and wisdom to know the difference.

*Reprinted with permission from Misery Addicts Anonymous.

Some details about how we conduct this meeting:

When we speak, we state our first name and own our addiction. For example, "Hi, I'm _____, and I'm a misery addict." Then we pause to be acknowledged by the others. If you are new to this meeting and you are unsure about your addiction, you can say, "Hi, I'm _____, and I have multiple addictions."

We are protected by the tradition of anonymity. People in recovery know they must speak the truth to get better. We ask you to honor our hospitality by not revealing the identities or stories of the people who are here.

We do not cross-talk at this meeting. Each person who shares, talks for her or his own recovery needs—not for the approval, acceptance, or entertainment of others. Please do not offer advice, comments, judgments, or reactions to another person's sharing.

Sometimes we laugh at tragic things. This comes from our joy in recovery and real relief that we aren't back where we were.

Feel free to share today. If you do not want to talk and someone calls on you, just say that you'd rather not talk today.

We are aware that some people suffer adverse respiratory reactions to perfume and scent, so please reduce or eliminate scent when you come to this meeting. Thank you.

Misery Addicts Anonymous is a fellowship of men and women who share their experience, strength, and hope with each other that they may solve their common problem and help others to recover from misery addiction. It is for anyone who is addicted to unhappiness, sadness, joylessness, isolation, avoidance, rebellion, or resistance, or anyone who is fearful of joy, success, happiness, intimacy, or well-being. The only requirement for membership is a desire to stop self-sabotage.

There are no dues or fees for MAA membership; we are self-supporting through our own contributions. MAA is not allied with any sect, denomination, political party, organization, or institution. It does not wish to engage in any controversy and neither endorses nor opposes any causes. Our primary purpose is to stay in recovery and to help other misery addicts maintain recovery.

I have asked _____ to read "How It Works." [This is read aloud.]

I have asked _____ to read the Twelve Traditions. [These are read aloud.]

If there is anyone here who considers themselves new to MAA, please introduce yourself by your first name only so that we can welcome you.

Are there any visitors?

Are there any MAA birthdays for the month of _____?

Who would like to volunteer to chair this meeting next week?

Are there any MAA announcements?

Are there any non-MAA announcements?

Later in the meeting we will pass the basket in keeping with the Seventh Tradition that every MAA group ought to be self-supporting.

We request that those wishing to share a second time wait until everyone else has had a chance to share.

Today is a

- Step Meeting and the Step is _____.
- Book Study and the book we are reading is _____.
- Speaker's Meeting and the speaker is _____.
- Topic Meeting.

If it is a Topic Meeting, introduce yourself again, then proceed with your own sharing about your experience, strength, or hope, ending with the topic for the day. You can call on people; you can have people share in order around the circle; or you can "play tag," calling on the first person and letting that person call on the next person. You can also ask if anyone has an urgent need and wants to go next. At some point during the meeting, pass the basket.

Closing the Meeting

Start closing the meeting five minutes before the published, official ending time. Following is a sample dialogue to close the meeting.

Does anyone have a burning desire to speak a second time?

Thank you all for being here. We hope to see you next week/next time. Remember that just by attending a meeting, you do a service to others. We couldn't have a meeting if you weren't here.

Remember, too, that anonymity, like recovery, is a treasured possession. What you hear here and who you see here, please leave here.

I have asked _____ to read the Twelve Promises from chapter 6 of *Alcoholics Anonymous.* [This is read aloud.]

Following that, we will form a circle and close with the Serenity Prayer. [Recite the Serenity Prayer together.]

HOW IT WORKS

Many Twelve Step meetings include a reading of "How It Works," which is taken from chapter 5 of *Alcoholics Anonymous* (the Big Book). The principles in that chapter still work, making a powerful statement about what is required for recovery.

What follows is a translation of "How It Works" for misery addicts.

1. We admitted we were powerless over self-sabotage—that our lives had become unmanageable.
2. Came to believe that a Power greater than ourselves could restore us to sanity.
3. Made a decision to turn our will and our lives over to the care of God as we understood God.
4. Made a searching and fearless moral inventory of ourselves.
5. Admitted to Our God, to ourselves, and to another human being the exact nature of our wrongs.
6. Were entirely ready to have Our God remove all these defects of character.
7. Humbly asked Our God to remove our shortcomings.
8. Made a list of all persons we had harmed, and became willing to make amends to them all.
9. Made direct amends to such people wherever possible, except when to do so would injure them or others.
10. Continued to take personal inventory and when we were wrong promptly admitted it.
11. Sought through prayer and meditation to improve our conscious contact with God as we understood God, praying only for knowledge of Our God's will for us and the power to carry that out.
12. Having had a spiritual awakening as the result of these steps, we tried to carry this message to misery addicts, and to practice these principles in all our affairs.

Many of us exclaimed, "What an order! I can't go through with it!" Do not be discouraged. No one among us has been able to maintain anything close to perfect adherence to these principles. We are not saints. The point is that we are willing to grow along spiritual lines. The principles we have set down are guides to progress. We claim spiritual progress rather than spiritual perfection.

Our description of the misery addict and our personal adventures before and after starting recovery make clear three pertinent ideas:

- That we were addicted to self-sabotage and avoidance and could not manage our own lives
- That probably no human power could have relieved our misery addiction
- That a Higher Power could and would relieve us of this addiction if that Power were sought

THE TWELVE TRADITIONS

These following traditions are adapted from the Twelve Traditions of Alcoholics Anonymous.

1. Our common welfare should come first; personal recovery depends upon MAA unity.
2. For our group purpose there is but one ultimate authority—a loving God as God may be expressed in our group conscience. Our leaders are but trusted servants; they do not govern.
3. The only requirement for MAA membership is a desire to stop self-sabotage.
4. Each group should be autonomous except in matters affecting other groups or MAA as a whole.
5. Each group has but one primary purpose—to carry its message to the misery addict who still suffers.
6. An MAA group ought never endorse, finance, or lend the MAA name to any related facility or outside enterprise, lest problems of money, property, and prestige divert us from our primary purpose.
7. Every MAA group ought to be fully self-supporting, declining outside contributions.
8. Misery Addicts Anonymous should remain forever nonprofessional, but our service centers may employ special workers.
9. MAA, as such, ought never be organized; but we may create service boards or committees directly responsible to those they serve.
10. Misery Addicts Anonymous has no opinion on outside issues; hence, the MAA name ought never be drawn into public controversy.

11. Our public relations policy is based on attraction rather than promotion; we need always maintain personal anonymity at the level of press, radio, and films.

12. Anonymity is the spiritual foundation of all our traditions, ever reminding us to place principles before personalities.

ISSUES UNIQUE TO RECOVERY FROM A MISERY ADDICTION

"I Am a Misery Addict"

It is difficult to say "I am a misery addict" because we don't usually feel ourselves seeking misery. We may be more aware of avoiding things that scare us or an inertia that keeps us from acting sooner or more effectively.

At the beginning, you may only be able to say something such as "I am addicted to suffering," "I am addicted to self-sabotage," or "I am addicted to feeling bad."

It's all right to start there. However, in the long run, I believe you do yourself more good when you allow yourself to admit that you do have a misery addiction.

Here's why. Misery addicts tend to forget that what they are addicted to is a process, one that locks in almost automatically when they encounter a triggering event. Their avoidance system operates so mechanically that the trigger—a shaming comment, a glimpse into unbearable loneliness, a wave of unworthiness, a feeling of hopelessness—gets shrouded in denial instantly, dropping off the radar screen. From there, their system plays itself out using its usual techniques—a tool addiction, avoidance, resistance, rebellion, self-destructiveness, or isolation.

Thus the trigger vanishes, and no clear, single event stands as a marker in the cascade of setups, decisions, and nonactions that collapse in miserable consequences.

Misery addicts, as they slide downward, also forget the immediate consequences. As they reach for their tool addiction—the candy, the shopping cart, the Internet game—they are unconscious that the eventual outcome of this behavior will be to feel worse about themselves for yet again squandering their money, time, health, or opportunity.

Saying "I am a misery addict" is a powerful acknowledgment of two things—first, that you are addicted to a process, and second, that the consequence of that process is misery.

Birthdays (or Anniversaries)

Recovering alcoholics measure their birthdays (in many areas termed anniversaries) since the day after their last drink. This makes sense because it is necessary for alcohol and drug addicts to have a nonnegotiable standard of zero use since one slip could be the end of that addict's life.

But what constitutes an MAA birthday?

With misery addiction, all sorts of actions constitute self-sabotage. Nonaction can be self-sabotage too. Taking a break could be self-care in one circumstance and self-sabotage in another.

One hundred percent elimination of self-sabotaging actions and thoughts day in and day out is too much to expect. It would be self-sabotage to set a standard of such perfection. We can count on sabotaging ourselves again, at least occasionally. We are powerless, and we are human. To try to reach perfection would lure us into trying to control our addiction, thus pushing us away from Step One. In that direction lies failure. For us, the sign of recovery has to be our *response* to self-sabotage.

With misery addiction, we have to set the bar in a different place. We have to base birthdays on two things: ongoing contact with our recovery community and our response to self-sabotage.

Each person has a different process that leads to misery, so we each have to study our own life to define the particulars of our abstinence. We discuss this openly with people in our recovery community to avoid the dangers of fooling ourselves and to have help in identifying setups.

We find a place to start. We get help sorting through which manifestation of our addiction needs the most attention. We begin to work the program with one aspect of our lives in which we are hurting ourselves.

Abstinence will increase, bit by bit, as we begin to follow and live the process of recovery. Our consciousness will expand, and we will begin to see areas of stagnation that we are willing to examine and work with. Over time, we can work toward full abstinence.

Full abstinence for a misery addict includes the following:

- Consistently making efforts to recover from the misery addiction
- Responding immediately to any self-sabotage with recovery-related action
- Setting up positive outcomes, deliberately and in advance
- Participating in recovery programs around any tool addictions

Our birthday counting begins as soon as we put ourselves in a recovery community, and it continues to build as long as we stay in contact with such a community.

We do *not* lose our birthday if we make a mistake and lose ground. We only lose our birthday by not returning to the community after making a mistake. If we are making a lot of mistakes, then we keep our birthday as long as we increase our recovery contact to eliminate the increase in mistakes.

In other words, we treat birthdays as a way to measure our progress rather than to honor single, discrete events.

Misery addiction is a process. Recovery is a process.

Are Birthdays Necessary?

I think so. We deserve recognition that we've stayed with the program, especially from those who know how difficult it is.

Birthdays inspire others. I just attended the birthday celebration of a woman with twenty-eight years of recovery. I'm always struck by the humility of people with long-term recovery. They aren't arrogant about it— far from it. In fact, they feel that it is miraculous that their lives were snatched from the voracious jaws of addiction.

Abstinence

Since we must always be on guard against deceiving ourselves, I've defined the parameters for abstinence below. I suggest you use these at first, making individual exceptions only after discussing them with your sponsor.

- Consistently make efforts to recover from misery addiction
  1. For the first year, attend three meetings a week and talk to a sponsor five days a week.
  2. For the second to fifth years, attend two meetings a week and talk to a sponsor three days a week.
  3. For the rest of your life, attend at least one meeting a week and talk to a sponsor at least once a week.
  4. Increase your recovery activities whenever your stress increases.

- Respond immediately to self-sabotage with recovery-related action
  1. Recognize the self-sabotage.
  2. Make immediate contact with your recovery community.

3. Admit your self-sabotage to at least one other person.
4. Change the conditions that led to the self-sabotage.

Over time, after consistently working a program, self-sabotage will gradually decrease until it rarely happens.

Set Up Positive Outcomes, Deliberately and in Advance

- Daily Practice (see pages 196–198).
- Use one positive tool from your toolshed every day.
- Take good care of yourself; get sufficient sleep and nutrition and a reasonable amount of regular exercise.
- Stay conscious of your patterns and usual ways of setting yourself up.
- Use Opposite Action (see page 229).

Participate in Recovery Programs to Address Tool Addictions

Use other Twelve Step programs as resources for tool addictions and as backups if an MAA group isn't in the neighborhood. These programs include

- OA (Overeaters Anonymous)
- AA (Alcoholics Anonymous)
- NA (Narcotics Anonymous)
- CoDa (Co-Dependents Anonymous)
- FAA (Food Addicts Anonymous)
- GA (Gamblers Anonymous)
- SAA (Sex Addicts Anonymous)
- SLAA (Sex and Love Addicts Anonymous)
- Al-Anon (for people who have close relationships with an addict)

Prevent Serious Relapse

Ongoing contact with your recovery community is your best protection against relapse.

As you continue in recovery, things will start going better. You might begin to hesitantly trust that life can work for you now.

Then, when something goes wrong, that fragile belief can crack and topple you into "What's the use?" Your community can stop that fall and remind you that *bad things happen but they don't always happen.*

You will begin changing. The sense of core unworthiness will slowly shift. Deep inside, you will start to know of your own core goodness.

Into this tender newness, any shaming event or large, unexpected set-back can be very painful. You may lose your awareness that such events are always temporary, that they pass, especially with help.

If you were going along nicely and then suddenly hit a wall, the chances are good that someone else did something that triggered your shame, which then got swallowed in a big gulp of avoidance. Retrace your path, mentally reliving what happened just before everything changed so that you can become conscious of the trigger event; get comfort; and if neces-sary, make advance plans to avoid such triggers in the future. Then you can once again let yourself experience your own core goodness.

SPONSORSHIP

If you are asked to be a sponsor—and you are willing in your heart to make that commitment—consider the following:

Your job as a sponsor is to lend an ear, remind her of the Steps and principles, and support her in following the structure of recovery. You share your experience, strength, hope, wisdom, and tough love.

You can't save him if he's determined to crash. However, you can no-tice when he's headed for trouble, state your concern, and strongly urge him to go a meeting.

You aren't her therapist, but you can encourage her to call her therapist.

There are many good books on recovery from addiction. Encourage him to read and talk to you about what he has read. Books on other addic-tions have a lot to offer, so be open to helpful literature from AA, OA, and recovery publishing houses such as Hazelden and Gürze Books.

Author Letter to Therapists

I hope your cranial lightbulbs have been popping on as you've read this book. By now, you've likely identified the clients in your practice who are addicted to misery.

No wonder it's been slow going with them. A client addicted to misery can make us feel like we missed some critical class when we were being educated—the one called "What to do when nothing works."

If at times you've feared you've lost your touch, do not worry. You've just been up against a person's survival system. You assumed, like I did for many years, that the person was coming to therapy because she wanted her life to improve.

Actually, she *does* want her life to improve. But even more, she wants to feel safe and to have the internal dialogue that paralyzes her to be comprehended. She wants to be with someone who understands what's going on for her.

I have an essay written just for you on my Web site. In it you'll find what I've learned about what works and what is doomed to fail in inter-actions with a client who is addicted to misery or self-sabotage. Included are suggestions for therapy goals, typical dilemmas faced by this client, how to respond to those dilemmas, mistakes to avoid, and examples from my own experience. I also answer the question: does a misery addict have a borderline personality disorder?

A client who is addicted to misery needs a different therapeutic struc-ture than an ordinary client. Indeed, I'll go so far as to say that expecting misery addicts to profit from a one-size-fits-all approach helps to set them up for more misery. Sadly, it also discourages them from therapy, one of the few venues that can show them (in concert with a recovery program) a way out of their desolation.

You are important to your client. Yet this client, more than many others, may tax your patience and require much of you. Perhaps my suggestions will allow you to relax, take a wider view, see this client more deeply, and embrace what matters most.

Please visit my Web site, www.annekatherine.com, for some support and ideas.

APPENDIX C

Resources

Misery Addicts Anonymous (MAA)
www.miseryaddicts.org
MAA
P.O. Box 1732
Coupeville, WA 98239
360-710-5362

Alcoholics Anonymous (AA)
www.alcoholics-anonymous.org
Alcoholics Anonymous World Services, Inc.
Grand Central Station
P.O. Box 459
New York, NY 10163
212-870-3400

Al-Anon
www.al-anon.alateen.org
Al-Anon Family Group Headquarters, Inc.
1600 Corporate Landing Parkway
Virginia Beach, VA 23454-5617
888-4AL-ANON

Co-Dependents Anonymous (CoDA)
www.codependents.org
Co-Dependents Anonymous, Inc.
P.O. Box 33577
Phoenix, AZ 85067-3577
602-277-7991

Food Addicts Anonymous (FAA)
www.foodaddictsanonymous.org
Food Addicts Anonymous World Service Office
4623 Forest Hill Blvd., Suite #109-4
West Palm Beach, FL 33415-9120
561-967-3871

Gamblers Anonymous (GA)
www.gamblersanonymous.org
Gamblers Anonymous
International Service Office
P.O. Box 17173
Los Angeles, CA 90017
213-386-8789

Narcotics Anonymous (NA)
www.na.org
Narcotics Anonymous World Services, Inc.
P.O. Box 9999
Van Nuys, CA 91409
818-773-9999

Overeaters Anonymous (OA)
www.overeatersanonymous.org
World Service Office of Overeaters Anonymous
P.O. Box 44020
Rio Rancho, NM 87174-4020
505-891-2664

Sex Addicts Anonymous (SAA)
www.sexaa.org
Independent Service Office of Sex Addicts Anonymous
P.O. Box 70949
Houston, TX 77270
800-477-8191

Sex and Love Addicts Anonymous (SLAA)
www.slaafws.org
Sex and Love Addicts Anonymous
Fellowship-Wide Services, Inc.
P.O. Box 338
Norwood, MA 02062-0338
781-255-8825

APPENDIX D

Notes

CHAPTER THREE

1. Martin Seligman, *Authentic Happiness* (New York: Free Press, 2002), 40.

CHAPTER SIX

1. Daniel Siegel, *The Developing Mind* (New York: Guilford Press, 1999), 24.
2. Ibid.
3. Ibid., 25.
4. B. Milner, L. R. Squire, and E. R. Kandel, "Cognitive Neuroscience and the Study of Memory," *Neuron* 20 (1998): 445–468.
5. Siegel, *Developing Mind*, 25.
6. Ibid., 26; D. O. Hebb, *The Organization of Behavior: A Neuropsychological Theory* (New York: Wiley, 1949), 70.

CHAPTER SEVEN

1. Daniel Siegel, *The Developing Mind* (New York: Guilford Press, 1999), 36–37.
2. Ibid., 30; D. N. Stern, *The Interpersonal World of the Infant* (New York: Basic Books, 1985), 90–94.
3. Siegel, *Developing Mind*, 31.

CHAPTER FIFTEEN

1. Jeremy Holmes, "Something There Is That Doesn't Love a Wall," in *Attachment Theory*, ed. Susan Goldberg et al. (Hillsdale, N.J.: Analytic Press, 2000), 26.

2. Mary Ainsworth et al., *Patterns of Attachment: A Psychological Study of the Strange Situation* (New Jersey: Lawrence Erlbaum Associates, 1978), 31–44.

3. Many of the following studies contributed to the information summarized in this chapter. These studies are described in detail in Susan Goldberg, ed. et al., *Attachment Theory* (Hillsdale, N.J.: Analytic Press, 2000), 45–84, 153–183, 407–467.

4. Ainsworth et al., *Patterns of Attachment*; Mary Main, "Recent Studies in Attachment," in Goldberg, 416.

5. Ainsworth et al., *Patterns of Attachment*; Mary Main, "Recent Studies in Attachment," in Goldberg, 416.

6. Peter Fonagy et al., "Attachment, the Reflective Self, and Borderline States," in Goldberg, 269.

7. H. R. Schaffer and P. E. Emerson, "The Development of Social Attachments in Infancy," *Monographs for the Society of Research in Child Development* in Inge Bretherton, "The Origins of Attachment Theory: John Bowlby and Mary Ainsworth," in Goldberg, 63.

8. Inge Bretherton, "The Origins of Attachment Theory," in Goldberg, 63.

9. Giovanni Liotti, "Disorganized/Dissociative Attachment in the Psychotherapy of the Dissociative Disorders," in Goldberg, 344.

10. Fonagy et al., "Attachment," in Goldberg, 248.

11. Ibid., 247.

12. Goldberg, *Attachment Theory*, 11.

13. Main, "Recent Studies," in Goldberg, 418.

14. Ibid.; except where noted, from this citation to the section entitled "Risk," all technical information regarding infant attachment behavior is based on studies reported by Main in Goldberg, 408–426.

15. Jude Cassidy and Phillip Shaver, *Handbook of Attachment: Theory, Research, and Clinical Applications* (New York: Guilford Press, 1999), 72.

16. Ibid.

17. Goldberg, *Attachment Theory*, 419.

18. Ibid., 35.

19. Main, "Recent Studies," in Goldberg, 423–424.

20. Ibid., 426.

21. Ibid., 426.

22. Nancy Weinfield et al., "The Nature of Individual Differences in

Infant-Caregiver Attachment," in Cassidy and Shaver, *Handbook of Attachment,* 69.

23. D. van den Boom, "Preventive Intervention and the Quality of Mother-Infant Interaction and Infant Exploration in Irritable Infants," in *Developmental Psychology Behind the Dikes,* ed. W. Koops et al. Amsterdam: Eburon, 249–270, in Goldberg, 160–161.

CHAPTER TWENTY

1. *Alcoholics Anonymous,* 3d ed. (New York: Alcoholics Anonymous World Services, 1976), 7.

CHAPTER TWENTY-ONE

1. Inge Bretherton, "The Origins of Attachment Theory," in Goldberg, 63.

CHAPTER TWENTY-TWO

1. *Twelve Steps and Twelve Traditions* (New York: Alcoholics Anonymous World Services, 1996), 21.

2. *The Twelve Steps and Twelve Traditions of Overeaters Anonymous* (Torrance, Calif.: Overeaters Anonymous, 1993), 1–2.

CHAPTER TWENTY-THREE

1. *The Twelve Steps and Twelve Traditions of Overeaters Anonymous* (Torrance, Calif.: Overeaters Anonymous, 1993), 9.

2. Joe McQ, *The Steps We Took* (Little Rock, Ark.: August House, 1990), 29.

3. *A Program for You* (Center City, Minn.: Hazelden, 1991), 70.

4. *Twelve Steps and Twelve Traditions* (New York: Alcoholics Anonymous World Services, 1996), 36.

5. *The Twelve Steps and Twelve Traditions of Overeaters Anonymous,* 19.

6. Stephanie Covington, *A Woman's Way through the Twelve Steps* (Center City, Minn.: Hazelden, 1994), 44–45.

CHAPTER TWENTY-FIVE

1. *A Program for You* (Center City, Minn.: Hazelden, 1991), 19.

CHAPTER TWENTY-SIX

1. Constance Wolfe, "Shame," lecture presented at Avonlea Retreat, Clinton, Wash. (January 2003).
2. Thanks to Constance Wolfe, M.S.W., for many parts of this process.

CHAPTER TWENTY-SEVEN

1. Thich Nhat Hanh, *Peace Is Every Step: The Path of Mindfulness in Everyday Life* (New York: Bantam, 1992), 10, 78–79.
2. Ibid., 57–58.
3. Ibid., 78.
4. Marshall Rosenberg, *Nonviolent Communication*ᔆᴹ: *A Language of Compassion* (Encinitas, Calif.: PuddleDancer Press, 1999), 6–7, 15–22, 26, 42, 52, 71, 97.
5. Ibid., 97–110.
6. Constance Wolfe, "Forgiveness in Recovery," keynote speech given at Recovery Conference, Residence XII, Bothel, Wash. (October 1988).

CHAPTER TWENTY-EIGHT

1. Sonata Bohen, "Your Amazing Brain," speech given at PESI HealthCare Seminar, Seattle, Wash. (March 2000).
2. Russell Blaylock, *Excitotoxins: The Taste That Kills* (Santa Fe: Health Press, 1997), xxi.
3. Ibid., 34.
4. Research by Dr. John Olney, reported in Blaylock, *Excitotoxins*, 37.
5. Blaylock, *Excitotoxins*, 19.
6. Ibid., 36.

APPENDIX E

References

Ainsworth, Mary, Mary C. Blehar, Everett Waters, and S. Wall. *Patterns of Attachment: A Psychological Study of the Strange Situation.* New Jersey: Lawrence Erlbaum Associates, 1978.

Alcoholics Anonymous. 3d ed. New York: Alcoholics Anonymous World Services, 1976.

Blaylock, Russell. *Excitotoxins: The Taste That Kills.* Santa Fe: Health Press, 1997.

Bohen, Sonata. "Your Amazing Brain." Speech given at PESI HealthCare Seminar, Seattle, Wash. (March 2000).

Bowlby, John. *Attachment.* London: Penguin, 1969.

Cassidy, Jude, and Phillip Shaver. *Handbook of Attachment: Theory, Research, and Clinical Applications.* New York: Guilford Press, 1999.

Covington, Stephanie. *A Woman's Way through the Twelve Steps.* Center City, Minn.: Hazelden, 1994.

Edwards, Betty. *Drawing on the Right Side of the Brain.* New York: J. P. Tarcher, 1989.

Fonagy, Peter, et al. "Attachment, the Reflective Self, and Borderline States." In *Attachment Theory,* edited by Susan Goldberg et al. Hillsdale, N.J.: Analytic Press, 2000.

Gawain, Shakti. *Creative Visualization.* California: New World Library, 2002.

Goldberg, Susan, ed., et al. *Attachment Theory.* Hillsdale, N.J.: Analytic Press, 2000.

Hanh, Thich Nhat. *Peace Is Every Step: The Path of Mindfulness in Everyday Life.* New York: Bantam, 1992.

Harbin, Thomas. *Beyond Anger—A Guide for Men: How to Free Yourself from the Grip of Anger and Get More Out of Your Life.* New York: Marlowe and Company, 2000.

Hebb, D. O. *The Organization of Behavior: A Neuropsychological Theory.* New York: Wiley, 1949.

Katherine, Anne. *Anatomy of a Food Addiction.* Carlsbad, Calif.: Gürze Books, 1991.

———. *Boundaries: Where You End and I Begin.* Center City, Minn.: Hazelden, 1991.

———. *Where to Draw the Line.* New York: Simon and Schuster, 2000.

Katz, Lawrence, Manning Rubin, and David Suter. *Keep Your Brain Alive.* New York: Workman, 1999.

Liotti, Giovanni. "Disorganized/Dissociative Attachment in the Psychotherapy of the Dissociative Disorders." In *Attachment Theory,* edited by Susan Goldberg et al. Hillsdale, N.J.: Analytic Press, 2000.

Main, Mary. "Recent Studies in Attachment." In *Attachment Theory,* edited by Susan Goldberg et al. Hillsdale, N.J.: Analytic Press, 2000.

McQ, Joe. *The Steps We Took.* Little Rock, Ark.: August House, 1990.

Milner, B., L. R. Squire, and E. R. Kandel. "Cognitive Neuroscience and the Study of Memory." *Neuron* 20 (1998): 445–468.

A Program for You. Center City, Minn.: Hazelden, 1991.

Rosenberg, Marshall. *Nonviolent Communication^SM: A Language of Compassion.* Encinitas, Calif.: PuddleDancer Press, 1999.

Schaffer, H. R., and P. E. Emerson. "The Development of Social Attachments in Infancy." *Monographs for the Society of Research in Child Development* 94, no. 29 (1963). In *Attachment Theory,* edited by Susan Goldberg et al. Hillsdale, N.J.: Analytic Press, 2000.

Seligman, Martin. *Authentic Happiness.* New York: Free Press, 2002.

Semmelroth, Carl, and Donald Smith, *The Anger Habit.* Nashville, Tenn.: Writer's Showcase Press, 2000.

Siegel, Daniel. *The Developing Mind.* New York: Guilford Press, 1999.

Stern, D. N. *The Interpersonal World of the Infant.* New York: Basic Books, 1985.

Twelve Steps and Twelve Traditions. New York: Alcoholics Anonymous World Services, 1996.

The Twelve Steps and Twelve Traditions of Overeaters Anonymous. Torrance, Calif.: Overeaters Anonymous, 1993.

Wolfe, Constance. "Forgiveness in Recovery." Keynote speech given at Recovery Conference, Residence XII, Bothel, Wash. (October 1988).

———. "Shame." Lecture presented at Avonlea Retreat, Clinton, Wash. (January 2003).

Index

About the Author

For thirty years, Anne Katherine has been shepherding clients into the inner spaces that hold the forgotten wounds and hidden sorrows that shape a person's perceptions and choices. She has developed programs for food addicts (Full Heart, Full Belly) and discovery of life purpose (Soul Path).

Now Anne Katherine has created a very effective recovery program for women addicted to misery and self-sabotage (Escape from Suffering). She has also founded Avonlea, a nonprofit recovery center, and Misery Addicts Anonymous.

Anne Katherine is a licensed mental health counselor, a board certified regression therapist, a certified eating disorders specialist, and a registered hypnotherapist. Find Anne at www.annekatherine.com.

OTHER BOOKS BY ANNE KATHERINE

Boundaries: Where You End and I Begin
Anatomy of a Food Addiction
Where to Draw the Line